LIBERATION PREACHING

LIBERATION PREACHING
.
The Pulpit and the Oppressed

Justo L. González
and
Catherine Gunsalus González

ABINGDON PREACHER'S LIBRARY
William D. Thompson, Editor

ABINGDON
Nashville

Liberation Preaching: The Pulpit and the Oppressed

Copyright © 1980 by Abingdon

Library of Congress Cataloging in Publication Data

GONZÁLEZ, JUSTO L.
    Liberation preaching.
    (Abingdon preacher's library)
    Bibliography: p.
    Includes index.
    1. Preaching. 2. Liberation theology. 3. Bible—Criticism, interpretation, etc. I. Gunsalus González, Catherine, joint author. II. Title.
BV4211.2.G65   251   79-27858

ISBN 0-687-21700-8

MANUFACTURED BY THE PARTHENON PRESS AT
NASHVILLE, TENNESSEE, UNITED STATES OF AMERICA

To each other

CONTENTS

LIST OF ABBREVIATIONS

BAC	Biblioteca de Autores Cristianos
KJ	The Bible, King James Version
PG	Patrologia Graeca (Migne)
PL	Patrologia Latina (Migne)
RSV	The Bible, Revised Standard Version
TEV	The Bible, Today's English Version

EDITOR'S FOREWORD

Preaching has captured the attention of increasingly large segments of the American public. Lay parish committees seeking pastoral leadership consistently rank preaching as the most desirable pastoral skill. Seminary courses and clergy conferences on preaching attract participants in larger numbers than ever. Millions of viewers watch television preachers every week.

What is *good* preaching? is the question of both those who hear it and those who do it. Hearers answer that question instinctively, tuning in the preacher who meets their needs, whether in the pulpit of the neighborhood church or on a broadcast. Preachers need to answer more intentionally.

Time was that a good, thick book on preaching would do it, or a miscellaneous smattering of thin ones. The time now seems ripe for a different kind of resource—a carefully conceived, tightly edited series of books whose scope covers the homiletical spectrum and whose individual volumes reveal the latest and best thinking about each specialty within the field of preaching. The volumes in the Abingdon Preacher's Library enable the preacher to understand preaching in its historical setting; to examine its biblical and theological underpinnings; to explore its spiritual, relational, and liturgical dimensions; and to develop insights into its craftsmanship.

Designed primarily for use in the seminary classroom, this series will also serve the practicing preacher whose background in homiletics is spotty or out-of-date, or whose preaching needs strengthening in some specific area.

William D. Thompson
Eastern Baptist Theological Seminary
Philadelphia, Pennsylvania

I. WHAT IS LIBERATION THEOLOGY?

The North American theological scene has a tendency to latch on to key words and phrases, as if their use were proof that one is up to date. A few years ago it was "secularity." Later it was the "death of God." Today it is "liberation." Preachers of all shades of opinion speak of liberation. Every ecclesiastical assembly seems to feel compelled to include it in its pronouncements. It would seem that one cannot go wrong as long as one is for "liberation."

But words, like coins, lose their sharpness when they are overused. At that point, all sorts of counterfeits are possible. This became clear when the Roman Catholic Church in Latin America was preparing for the Bishops' Conference which took place in Puebla in 1979. At that point, many of the most belligerent opponents of liberation theology employed the strategy of coopting the term "liberation" and interpreting it in their own conservative fashion.[1] Therefore, before we proceed to deal with the subject of liberation preaching, we must clarify what is meant in this context by "liberation theology."

POWER AND POWERLESSNESS: A MATTER OF PERSPECTIVE

When we speak here of "liberation theology," we are referring to theology done from the perspective of those who have been traditionally powerless in society and voiceless in the church. In the United States, this means blacks, Hispanics, Asian Americans, and others. In Latin America, Asia, and Africa, it means those who have long been the subjects of colonialism, economic and political as well as ecclesiastical. In societies which worship youth, it means the aged. All over the world, it means women.

There is a growing number of people in these groups who have rejected the self-image imposed on them. If one takes as an example the case of international colonialism, it has been shown that the colonizers need to justify their enterprise by developing a theory of their cultural superiority, and selling that view to the colonized. For a while, overwhelmed by the power of the colonizers, generations of the colonized may believe what they are told about themselves—their lack of responsibility and organizational skills, their emotionalism, their lack of cultural creativity, etc. But eventually, through a process which takes different shapes in various situations, they come to the realization that they do not have to accept the self-image which has been imposed on them by the colonizers.[2] This process, which has spelled the death of the international colonial empires of the nineteenth century, is also taking place in societies such as ours among those who have been those societies' internal colonies—blacks, chicanos, Asian Americans, Native Americans, and women. It is on the toil of such people, and of the colonized overseas, that the great wealth of the North Atlantic has been built. And yet those people receive the smallest share of that wealth. Therefore, the change in self-image on their part is not a purely psychological or internal matter, but one which demands basic structural changes in the ordering of our society.

Not all people who have come to this awareness belong to the church. Many have left it because they perceive it as part of the structure of oppression against which they must rebel. And we must admit that such a view is amply justified, when we remember how Christianity was used to take land from Native Americans and then from Mexicans, how it justified slavery, how few Christian leaders protested against the internment of Japanese Americans during the Second World War, and how the Bible has been used to keep women in a subservient role. At the same time, there are many members of these groups who, out of their Christian faith, refuse to join the movement toward a new self-image or to demand their rights. Many have been taught that it is unchristian to rock the boat or that if they are humble here on earth they will be rewarded in heaven or that they should be content to be of service to others and not claim positions of leadership.

Therefore, not all those who are involved in the various liberation movements can be called liberation *theologians,* for many have rejected all Christian theology as oppressive. Likewise, not all members of these groups who do theology can be called *liberation* theologians, for many simply repeat and reflect what they have been taught by others.

Liberation theology is that done from the perspective of the traditionally powerless as they experience the empowerment of the gospel, not only in an inner sense, but also in the sense that it compels and enables them to strive for justice. In rejecting the traditional interpretation of the Christian message, they refuse to leave the gospel in the hands of the powerful, to be used for their purposes, and insist that a proper interpretation of Scripture is freeing rather than oppressive.

This is not to say that the powerful have deliberately set out to interpret the Bible in an oppressive way. The truth is much more subtle than that. What actually takes place is an unconscious process through which the values, goals, and interests of those in power are read into Scripture.

Take for instance what happened in the early centuries of the Christian church. At first, most Christians belonged to the lower classes. Their opponents said that they were uncouth and unlearned, and that their teaching made no sense. A great deal of the Christian literature of the first four centuries seeks to respond to that challenge by showing that Christianity agrees with the best of Greek philosophy and Roman law. As an effort to communicate the gospel to those outside the church, this response is quite understandable. But what eventually took place was that Christians themselves began to think that Greek philosophy and Roman law spoke a clearer word about God and the divine purposes than did the Bible itself. By the time Constantine came to power, in the early fourth century, and he and his successors embraced Christianity, it was possible to do so without rejecting many of the values of the "best" Graeco-Roman society.

The conversion of Constantine, and the support which most of his successors gave to the church, accelerated the process. Eusebius of Caesarea wrote a *Church History* which made it appear that the only reasons why the empire had persecuted the church were grave misunderstandings and the maliciousness of some rulers—when in fact many of those who led the worst persecutions were among the ablest statesmen and most just rulers who ever governed the empire. The book of Revelation, which spoke of Rome in rather uncomplimentary fashion, was shunned, and Eusebius himself had doubts about its inclusion in the canon of the New Testament.[3] The ritual of Christian worship began to imitate the formalities of the imperial court, with all their distinctions between various levels in the civil hierarchy. Christ was depicted as sitting on a heavenly throne, in a posture which resembled that of the emperors on their thrones. Even the cross was often studded with precious gems. Anything to obscure the fact that the One whom the church worshiped was a poor carpenter from Galilee, who had been condemned to death as an outlaw by Roman authorities.

Again, this was not a conscious process. Indeed, when one reads the documents of the time one comes across repeated protestations that what is being taught and done in the church is exactly what the apostles taught and did. The "faith of the fathers" became the watchword of orthodoxy. But the "fathers" were for the most part seen as bishops who sat on thrones, very much like the Emperor in Constantinople and the images of Christ in heaven.

There were protests against this. The Donatists broke away from the church and eventually were put down by sheer military force. At another level, the development of monasticism was also a sort of protest. Since the church had embraced the values of the surrounding society, these women and men (in Egypt there seem to have been twice as many female monastics as there were male) felt that the best way for them to reject those values was to live in seclusion, preferably in the desert. This feeling was so widespread that soon travelers said that the desert was as populated as a city. Others, while embracing the monastic attitude toward the prevailing values of society, continued their active involvement in the life of the church and often collided with the powerful. These were the great saints of the fourth and fifth centuries: Athanasius, Ambrose, Jerome, Macrina, Basil, John Chrysostom, etc. Many of these we shall have occasion to quote later on, when we deal with the resources for liberation preaching from the early Christian tradition.

The usually unconscious process of adapting Christian teaching to the views and interests of the powerful did not end with Constantine and his successors. It has continued, for instance, in the manner in which the oppression and persecution of Jews has received religious and theological sanction. In the history of the Western Hemisphere it has appeared again and again in the taking of the land from its original inhabitants, in the destruction of ancient civilizations, in the annexation of Mexican territories by the U.S., in black slavery on both continents, etc., etc.

This oppressive use of supposedly Christian doctrine has repeatedly been pointed out. However, what we often fail to realize is that most of the people who did this were sincere in their beliefs. It is not that they consciously decided to interpret the Bible in such a way that it supported exploitation. It is rather that, from their perspective, a different interpretation was highly unlikely. And, since their views were reflected in the centers of authority within the church, their interpretation became normative and was passed on as authoritative, not only to later generations among the powerful, but also to the powerless, who were left with the alternative of either acquiescing to exploitation or rejecting Christianity.

What is happening with the birth of liberation theologies is that many among the traditionally powerless are asking the basic question of whether or not the manner in which the Bible has been interpreted by the powerful is accurate. This is the "ideological suspicion" of which we shall have much more to say later on. Could it not be that a biblical interpretation, so to speak, "from below" would uncover dimensions of the biblical message that have often been ignored?

THE MAIN BIBLICAL PERSPECTIVE

Many have argued that an interpretation of the Bible done by the powerless would be no less biased and determined by self-interest than is the current one done by the powerful. Why trade one such interpretation for another? Nothing would really be gained. The response of liberation theologians is clear at this point and needs to be understood before any real progress can be made in the appreciation of liberation theology for preaching. It has to do with the perspective of the Bible itself.

If the major portion of the Bible is written by those who, in their own social situation, are the powerless and oppressed, if it is their perspective on the activity of God that is given us by Scripture, then surely a more accurate interpretation of the biblical word can be gained by those who currently stand in a parallel place in our own societies than by those who are powerful. This response needs to be looked at in some detail.

First of all, is it true that most of the Bible is written from the perspective of the powerless? Surely this is the case. The people of Israel begin their organized life as a band of runaway slaves, escaping the oppression of Pharaoh. Even the Promised Land they finally attain is an insecure piece of geography, at the crossroads of trade routes and constantly a battleground for the mighty empires that surround Israel. The only times Israel has a semblance of independent national life is in brief periods when these empires—Egypt to the west, or whatever is the current name of the peoples to the northeast in the great Mesopotamian and Persian area, and finally Macedonia, Syria, and Rome—are in disarray internally and cannot exercise their usual demand for tribute or subservience.

Almost perversely, God chose a people weak and small in number in preference to the mighty nations of the earth (Deut. 7:7). Part of the reason for this is that Israel could then be clear that the power is God's power, and not Israel's own strength (Deut. 8:1-20). In grateful response to God, Israel ought then to be obedient to God's will as expressed in the law. Relying on her own strength, which was tempting whenever the nation seemed to be strong and independent, inevitably brought about faithlessness and disobedience, which God then punished and cured by removing Israel's apparent power.

The slaves escaping from Egypt surely had a different perspective on God's activity and character than did their Egyptian pursuers. The kings of Israel often forgot the Law when the nation was strong and prosperous. Even mighty David was rebuked by Nathan the prophet (II Sam. 12:1-15). David's greatness was seen in his response to the rebuke, in his hearing of the Word of God to him from the prophet. Other kings did not listen so well. King Jeroboam much preferred to listen to his own court priests who told him what he wished to hear than to Amos, the rough shepherd from out of town, who brought God's authentic word to him (Amos 7:10-17).

This is the pattern throughout much of the Old Testament. The powerful nations are overthrown by small Israel when Israel is obedient. The powerful within Israel are rebuked by the seemingly powerless prophets. What is astonishing is that the Old Testament records all of this. The Old Testament is not only our sacred Scripture. It is also a national history. Such histories normally glorify the nation. All difficulties are due to evil enemies, never to sinfulness within the nation itself. National heroes are models of perfection and their weaknesses overlooked. That is the general plan of secular national histories. But the Old Testament is quite different, and in this difference is seen the revelation of God. The official records are included, but the minority report of the prophets is even more in evidence. What has been preserved by Israel is the perspective of the powerless over against the viewpoint of the powerful. Included also are the repentant powerful who have learned through their own bitter experience that God is the defender of the poor and oppressed and not the supporter of the unjust, whether they be kings or nations.

Yet this does not mean that God prefers those who maintain a low opinion of themselves. Too often humility has been interpreted in this manner. Rather, God seems to choose those who have been made to feel like outcasts, those who are powerless and marginal, and then gives them a new sense of self-worth. God vindicates them in the eyes of their former oppressors. This theme of vindication of the powerless is a constant one in the Old Testament (see especially I Sam. 2:1-10). It is to be contrasted with the sinful arrogance of the powerful who believe themselves secure in their own strength (see Ps. 73). Humility and weakness alone are not enough for faithfulness. In the Old Testament, faithful humility is combined in the powerless with the belief that God will indeed be their strength and that they can therefore hold their heads up very high, especially in the face of their oppressors.

In the New Testament, we are not dealing with a national history, but rather with that of an emerging institution. Yet the same pattern continues. Those who hear the gospel gladly are by and large not the powerful within the society of Israel. Rather, they are the fisherfolk, the women, the poor, and those who are marginalized because of their occupations: the tax collectors and the harlots.

The early church, as it moved into Gentile circles, continued to attract those who were unimportant and even powerless, rather than the elite among the Greeks (I Cor. 1:26-31). Yet there were some exceptions. Within Judaism, and within the New Testament, Paul is the major one who comes from the situation of the powerful. He was clearly among the educated and respected within Judaism (Phil. 3:4-6). We know also that Paul was a Roman citizen, which gave him status within the empire itself. Paul can be classified among the "repentant powerful," rather like King David. For him, believing in this "nobody" Jesus meant joining a group that was totally unlike his own insecure social position. He joined by deciding that the future lay with this marginal group and not with the trimmings of prestige and power to which he had been accustomed (Phil. 3:7-9).

Simon Magus is another example of a powerful person who becomes a Christian. But it takes the fisherman, Simon Peter, to make clear to him that his understanding of the faith is very faulty. Simon Magus evidently then repents and hears the gospel authentically (Acts 8:9-24), but the New Testament does not give us any glimpse into his life after this encounter, such as we are given into the life of Paul.

The New Testament, just as the Old, shows the people of God with all of their faults. We are not presented with an ideal group of perfect people. It is precisely the weakness of the people that allows the surpassing power of God to be seen. And when the people are faithful to such a God, these weak ones are filled with a power that astonishes even the powerful outside the church.

The supreme example of this is, of course, Jesus himself. In terms of worldly power and prestige, surely he was an outsider. Born in a stable while his parents were being moved around by an alien government; the child of poor parents, he grew up in an obscure village where the mighty need not pay any attention to him! And yet, in this One, God was incarnate. It would have made more sense for the divine incarnation to be in the form of a king or a priest, or at least one of the elite of Jerusalem. Yet God the Son chose the form of a servant (Phil. 2:6-8), one of the powerless ones, even as God had chosen Israel, a weak nation. The cross shows the culmination of such a life, with all of its weakness and marginality. The resurrection shows the vindication by God in the most radical form.

God has a proclivity for speaking the word through the powerless. The whole Bible bears witness to this. Is this an accident, or is it an essential element of the gospel itself? Is there something about God's word that can best be heard and spoken by the powerless? Liberation theology would say there is indeed. And in this it is supported by the words of Jesus: "I thank thee, Father, . . . that thou hast hidden these things from the wise and understanding and revealed them to babes" (Luke 10:21). The powerful have a difficult time hearing God accurately. Their choice seems to be hearing God's word to them through some apparently powerless person—Nathan, Amos, Simon Peter, Jesus—or not hearing it at all. Such theology would say also that in our own day, this pattern continues. The powerless have readier access to an authentic understanding of the gospel than do the powerful. The powerful need to hear the word through voices they have rejected in their own society. Liberation theology is an understanding of the gospel arising precisely in the midst of such traditionally rejected voices.

SOME BASIC TRAITS AND THEMES

Since the theologies of liberation coming out of diverse groups and situations reflect the concreteness of the struggle in which they are involved, there is no such thing as a "general" or "universal" theology of liberation. And yet, there are some common traits.

The first of these is that all theologies of liberation are politically concrete. They do not seek to be universal, for they know by bitter experience that what is usually called "universal" is too often the projection of the values, self-image, and interest of a powerful group. In a white racist society an "average" human being is depicted as white. In a sexist society, male domination seems normal, and males take for granted that the fruit of their philosophical and theological reflection has nothing to do with their gender or position of dominance.

This emphasis on concreteness and particularity appears in the various theologies of liberation. Mexican theologian Raúl Vidales has said that "There has never been a 'universal' theology, and even less has there existed a neutral one."[4] Likewise, James H. Cone states that "Black theologians must work in such a way as to destroy the corruptive influence of white thought by building theology on the sources and norms that are appropriate to the black community."[5] Therefore, although there are many points of contact, and certainly a common perspective, joining the various theologies of liberation, it is important to keep in mind this emphasis on concreteness, in order to avoid the temptation of becoming a preacher of a universal liberation theology or of someone else's liberation—which is what easily happens when some white males decide to preach liberation.

A second common characteristic of liberation theologies is that the main category with which they work is that of history. A significant segment of traditional theology deals with truth, understood in terms of changelessness and universality. Others seem to believe that the basic category of the biblical message is that of law, doing what is proper and orderly. But liberation theologians know that supposedly "universal" truth is too often the projection of the particular views and interests of the powerful, that changelessness is a value espoused by those who benefit from the status quo, for whom change would be threatening, and that law is most cherished by those who have the civil law and order on their side. As we read the Bible, what we see in it is not so much a book of eternal truths, nor a book of rules, as a book of history. In the Bible, truth is not something that "is," in the sense in which Parmenides used that word, but rather something that happens. And laws are given, not to stifle that happening, but to foster it. This is why Cone says that "In the Bible revelation is inseparable from history and faith. History is the arena in which God's revelation takes place."[6] And Letty M.

Russell speaks both for feminist theology and for other theologies of liberation when she asserts that "Most liberation theologies are written from the modern point of view that both humanity and the world are to be understood as historical, as both changing and changeable."[7]

This understanding of history, however, has to be clarified. History is not simply the narration of past events. History is a project, both divine and human, for the redemption of God's creation. "If theology is really to speak meaningfully about the mediating point between the 'is' and the 'ought' of human life," says a feminist theologian, "then it takes as its base the entire human project."[8] And Gustavo Gutiérrez: "Indeed, if human history is above all else an opening to the future, then it is a task, a political occupation, through which man orients and opens himself to the gift which gives history its transcendent meaning: the full and definitive encounter with the Lord and with other men."[9] James Cone agrees: "By making revelation a historical happening, the Bible makes faith something other than an ecstatic feeling in moments of silent prayer, or an acceptance of inerrant propositions. Faith is the community's response to God's act of liberation. It is saying Yes to God and No to oppressors."[10]

A third common characteristic of liberation theologies might appear at first glance to be at odds with what has just been said. Liberation theology refuses to limit itself to the themes most directly and obviously connected with its struggles. This is one of its most puzzling characteristics for those who look at it from the outside. Liberation theology is not a theology *about* liberation which is then content to leave all the other theological themes to traditional theology. On the contrary, it is convinced that its insights have a bearing on every single doctrine of the Christian faith, and that it is therefore a legitimate theology. "Feminist theology is *not* about women. It is about God."[11] And "when black people sing, preach, and tell stories about their struggle, one fact is clear: they are not dealing simply with themselves. . . . It is this affirmation of transcendence that prevents Black Theology from being reduced merely to the cultural history of the black people."[12]

For this reason, liberation theology deals with every theme in

Christian theology, from the doctrine of God to that of the last things.[13] But it deals with each and all of these themes from the perspective of its particular struggle and action—what some liberation theologians call "praxis."

It is obviously impossible to discuss here all the themes with which liberation theology deals. But in order to illustrate them, we shall deal very briefly with three of them: the doctrine of God, anthropology, and eschatology.

All liberation theologians are agreed that the God of the Bible is not the impassible, ineffable, immutable One of so much of traditional theology. Involved in their particular struggles as they are, they experience faith in a God who is active, who is involved with them in the struggle. This is the meaning that they see in the biblical phrase, "the living God"—a meaning which is amply supported by the incarnation of God in Christ. Out of that *praxis*, of that faith in action, they reflect both on the God of Scripture and the God of traditional theology and come to the conclusion that the impassible and ineffable One, far from being a better way to speak about the God of Scripture, is an idol. It is an idol of changelessness developed, albeit unwittingly, by those who are threatened by change, because the present order works in their favor. Liberation theologians can then point out that the philosophers who inspired this understanding of the Godhead were the same who boasted that philosophy was "the occupation of the idle," which obviously means those who, because of their social standing, do not have to work and do not wish to see that situation change. It is therefore not surprising that such philosophers produced, and bequeathed to later generations, a view of perfection as changelessness, and of change as that which threatens the very notion of perfection. In general, theologians who have followed the lead of such philosophers have been in similar social circumstances.

The fact that God is active also means that God is *not* neutral. This is the point which many find most disconcerting in liberation theology. They would prefer to speak of a God who deals with all in the same manner, like the blindfolded justice standing in front of our courthouses is supposed to do (although she appears to hear the sound of money and somehow seems to see people's color in spite of her blindfold!). But liberation theologians tell us that God did not deal equally with Pharaoh and with the children of Israel. God's justice is equalizing, because it is unequal. James Cone has said this in startling words: "Black theology cannot accept a view of God which does not represent him as being for blacks and thus against whites. Living in a world of white oppressors, black people have no time for a neutral God."[14]

God judges *for* the meek of the earth" (Isa. 11:4 emphasis added). It is this God, very different from the idol of our society, that liberation theologians discover in the midst of their struggle and in their theological reflection on that struggle.

If we then turn to anthropology, liberation theology rejects the notion that God is best served by our self-abasement. Too often has the Reformation doctrine of justification by faith been presented in such a manner. It is significant that many of those who tell us that humility is the greatest virtue, or that the root of all sin is pride, are doing so from prestigious pulpits and endowed chairs. The tone of the Bible is very different. There the beauty of creation is used to exalt God, and the human creature is seen as the crown of that creation (Ps. 8). Nowhere does the Bible tell us that we are called to be nothing. Rather, we are told that we are made after the divine image, that we are heirs of the Kingdom, children of God, priests and royalty. Any supposed humility that denies this is sinful, for it rejects the divine plan for creation. And yet, traditional theology has often been bent on promoting the virtue of humility, particularly since those who are humble will stay in their place and refuse to claim their rightful status in human societies as children and heirs of God.

Also, still in the realm of anthropology, liberation theologians are asking why is it that in so much preaching and teaching in the church "sin" is usually equated with an inner attitude, or at best with private misdeeds, and so seldom with the sort of sin most often condemned in the Bible, of "those who join house to house, who add field to field, until there is no more room" (Isa. 5:8). Why is it that our society, partly through the influence of Christian preaching, has practically come to equate sin with sexual disorders, while ignoring social injustice?[15] Could it not be that once again, and quite unwittingly, Christian theology has been serving the interests of the powerful?

Finally, when it comes to questions of eschatology, liberation theologies are showing that the understanding of "salvation" which has been bequeathed to us is rather truncated. The Bible deals much more with the kingdom of God and the Holy City, than with individual life after death. Life after death is part of the biblical message; however, in Scripture eternal life is usually placed within the context of a new social order. The Kingdom is not so much a place where all will be floating around in the presence of God, as a new order in which "they shall sit every man under his vine and under his fig tree, and none shall make them afraid" (Mic. 4:4). It is within that new order, the Kingdom, that eternal life takes place. Eternal life does not consist in being plucked out of history, but in being a participant in its culmination. In the present life, therefore, our task is to move toward that new order, to work for it, to announce it, and to train for it.

Again, this understanding of the goal of history has not been popular among the powerful because it would subvert the present order. As long as history and eternity are two parallel realms, with little relationship to each other, our task in history is to gain access to eternity—by being meek and accepting. But if history is part of eternity, and its purpose is to move toward the Kingdom, if the goal of history itself is that all shall sit under their own fig trees, it follows that our present system of land tenure must be revised. If salvation is seen as having one's soul go to heaven, those who exploit our bodies may even be seen as helps in that process. But if salvation is moving into a new order, which includes the entire human being, then we must strive against everything which at present denies that order.

Thus, at every point of Christian doctrine, liberation theology asks two basic questions: What does it really mean when we see it from the clearer vantage point of the oppressed? And, what is the hidden agenda in the interpretation which has been handed down to us?

LIBERATION AND THE TRAP OF PATERNALISM

If liberation theology is by definition theology done by those who have traditionally been powerless, how can it be useful to those who, by nationality, gender, race, or economic status, are to be classified as powerful? Most of the ministers in the main-line churches and most of the members of their congregations would be in that category. Can they appropriate and use such a theology without falsifying it? Can it speak to them as well as to the powerless?

There is great danger in the use of liberation theology by those who are generally thought of as the oppressors rather than the oppressed. It is one thing to find the gospel a liberating word to oneself. It is quite a different thing to believe ourselves agents for the liberation of others from a bondage we have never experienced. We are then in the position of announcing the power of a gospel for which we ourselves have no need in our own lives. Precisely because such agents of liberation have never actually experienced the bondage they now address, it is easy for them to oversimplify the problems and misunderstand the situation, both in its causes and in its cures. This can rapidly lead to frustration, especially if the easily seen cures do not work or are not accepted by those whom the agents seek to help.

Even more to the point, it is difficult to tell the role of "liberating agents" from traditional oppression. Such a role implicitly involves a sense of knowing what is good for the oppressed group, and the feeling that they are unable to advance without us. This role may actually be an unconscious cover for a continuation of earlier domination, though now with a more acceptable, "liberation" rhetoric employed. It involves little change in the underlying structures of power. Needless to say, the various liberation movements are suspicious of such agents. It is a significant thing for a black to help other blacks to be aware of their oppression and to take steps to work against domination by whites. It is significant when a woman helps other women to see and work against the domination of men. But for a white or a man to play the role of liberating agent is another matter entirely. The response of the oppressed group will probably be that the contribution of the traditionally powerful person may be helpful, but only in a supportive role, not in a leadership or even in a diagnostic one. The response may also be that they could be of more use in their own group of whites or of men, working for a change in structures that would alter the distribution of power.

The response of liberation theology to such offers of assistance from the powerful will probably include the strange idea that part of the uselessness of the powerful is that they are not really very powerful at all. Many white, middle-class liberal Christians in this country readily and constantly feel a sense of guilt for their position of affluence in a world beset by problems of hunger and poverty. Obviously, there is ample reason for such a sense of guilt. Yet often such guilt leads to the conclusion that we are guilty because we voluntarily chose such affluence. We created the problem and we can therefore alter the situation. The feeling of guilt is acceptable to us as long as we can also have the sense that we, unlike the oppressed we wish to help, are free and independent members of society. We can decide to assist those who are downtrodden to help them attain the status we have. It is not so pleasant to think of ourselves as both guilty and powerless. The thought that the vast majority of us who see ourselves as free are really the captives of the same structures and forces that cause the poverty we wish to eliminate is difficult to accommodate. Yet this thought is essential if we are to see how liberation theology can relate to our preaching and to many of our churches.

This is not the same as to say that we are all oppressed in one way or another and thus we can be rid of our sense of guilt. That will not do at all, though such an attitude often occurs when we discover our own powerlessness. Nor is it legitimate to spiritualize the meaning of bondage and say that some of us are captives of poverty and others of sin, but ultimately we are all in the same situation. This would imply that we need not deal with our role as oppressors at all, since ultimately all are oppressed. The reality of racism and colonialism, and the evils of injustice must be dealt with. The sense of guilt on the consciences of the comfortable must be nurtured and not assuaged.

Yet the truth remains. We are not the free people we often think we are. The bondage under which we live is subtle, and we are sufficiently rewarded that we do not notice our lack of freedom. The structures that buy or lease land in the Third World and displace people, causing them to become part of the inhuman slums of the sprawling cities, are the same structures that govern much of our lives as well. From products to pricing, from values to self-images, from advertising to television programming, our lives and those of our children are determined in ways that would startle our great-grandparents. If we try to alter things we discover that even regulatory agencies and government itself are strongly influenced by these same interests. Change is neither easy nor always possible. Our own employment may well be governed or at least financed by the same systems, and if we cry out too loudly, we are made aware that it is not wise.

What does all of this have to do with liberation theology? If we take it seriously, it has a great deal. If we can become aware of the social, political, and economic systems that control our lives, we may then find ourselves on the same side of the struggle as those who are the outcasts of those systems. We can then speak from our own experience of bondage and of the problems and frustrations in seeking to be free. We can know what it means to come to consciousness about our own exploitation, even though we fully recognize that our bondage has been quite comfortable. Only then can we really seek to be free.[16] We can find ourselves learning about such struggles from those whom we charitably tried to help before. They can become our teachers, rather than we theirs. The poor, precisely because they are at the margins of the system, may well know more about its actual working than we who are kept within it. Within the church there is great possibility for such a conversation because the church has within its membership all races, economic groups, and social conditions, and is spread over the face of the earth. Yet our local congregations fail to take constant advantage of this truly catholic character of the church and, in their own congregational life, fail to reflect it.

Liberation theology is significant for us when we seek to become free from actual oppressive structures that bind us. Wherever we, who think ourselves powerful, find that we are, indeed, bound, such a theology can inspire us to have the courage to challenge and to act as the redeemed children of God, as those who are indeed not conformed to this world.

For most of us in this country, liberation theology, to be useful and authentic, demands a kind of double personality. Our consciences must continue to remind us of evil from which we benefit while others suffer. Our awareness of this must increase and not decrease. Our affluence, even though it hardly seems that in comparison to richer neighbors, still is more than our share of the world's resources. Besides this, however, most of us find ourselves in multiple roles. We are the powerful by race if we are white, yet among the powerless if we are women. We are part of a powerless group if we are in an ethnic minority, yet if we are well educated and employed, we join the powerful in that category. Even within the family structure, the child is often the last victim of those who have no one else over whom to rule and yet are oppressed themselves. Our tendency is to claim only one part of our identity, to think of ourselves always as part of an oppressed group or to think of ourselves always as the powerful. A much more creative dynamic is possible when we claim both parts of our identity, and the liberation given by the gospel can nurture a constant interior dialogue within our own lives. It can also open our lives to a far greater dialogue in the world around us. Then liberation theology can speak to us and to our congregations, making clear and judging our roles as oppressors, but also making clear and freeing us from whatever powers bind us, even those forces that bind us into the role of oppressors in the wider society.

II. DIFFICULTIES IN HEARING THE TEXT

Since the main task of the preacher of liberation is to listen anew to the biblical text, this chapter and the next two will deal with the question of biblical interpretation. In the present chapter, we shall discuss some of the obstacles which impede a liberating interpretation, and in the others we shall deal with some resources for overcoming those obstacles.

SOLA SCRIPTURA

One of the main principles of the Protestant Reformation was that of *sola Scriptura*—the sole authority of Scripture in questions of faith. The Reformers themselves did not agree on the scope and application of that principle. Some, like Luther, meant by it that anything which was contrary to the clear words of Scripture should be rejected, while traditions that did not contradict the Bible could—and normally should—be retained. Zwingli and others went much farther and sought to do away with anything that was not clearly supported by Scripture. But in spite of these differences, all agreed that the reason why the Reformation was needed was that, to a greater or lesser degree, the tradition of the church made it difficult, if not impossible, to read the Bible correctly. Thus, in a sense, the Reformation of the sixteenth century was an attempt to rediscover the biblical word, somehow obscured by its traditional interpretation.

As is well known, this gave rise to bitter controversy. It is difficult for us today to understand the real nature of that controversy, because we are told that it was simply a matter of the relative authority of tradition vis-à-vis Scripture, and at present both Protestants and Roman Catholics agree that there is a certain priority to Scripture. But those who opposed the Reformers in the sixteenth century did not see matters in this light. To them what was being attacked was not simply a tradition that was clearly distinct from the Bible. They were so used to reading the Bible as they had been taught by generations of interpreters that any questioning of that interpretation seemed to be a questioning of Scripture itself. Therefore the thrust of their argument was not, as has so often been said, that tradition was above Scripture, or that it was parallel to it, but rather that the two were so closely entwined that to doubt the traditional interpretation was to doubt the authority of both Bible and tradition.

This tendency to identify what Scripture says with what we have been told it says is one of the main obstacles in the way to a liberating interpretation of the Bible. This was brought home to us when we wrote a book on women in the Bible for the Presbyterian Church in the U. S. [1] The response of one of the conservative local churches was that they could not use our book because it "disagrees with the traditional interpretation of the Bible" regarding women. And this from a church that calls itself an heir to John Calvin!

What the women in that church did was precisely what was done by those who opposed the Reformers in the sixteenth century: they confused a tradition of interpretation with the text itself, without realizing that, if the interpretation can be substituted for the text, the latter has been made superfluous. But they also refused to recognize that such traditions of interpretation are not ideologically neutral. They do not just happen. On the contrary, they have an agenda. They reflect the perspectives and the interests of the interpreters. And they do this to a degree which is usually in inverse relation to the degree to which the interpreter is conscious of what is taking place. In other words, the less aware the interpreter is of his or her biases, the more surreptitiously they will permeate the interpretation. In the case of issues regarding women, for instance, the most insidious interpretations have not come from those who consciously set out to put women down, but rather from an entire tradition which developed in a society which took for granted that women were inferior human beings, and in which biblical interpreters—almost exclusively male—reflected that bias in their exposition of Scripture.

The first task of liberation theologians and preachers is to rid themselves of any undue burden of tradition. This is indeed difficult, for as Christians we affirm a *historic* faith, and this in turn means that ours is a faith that must have a tradition. We are heirs of the "Fathers," of medieval theologians, of the Reformers, and of the Puritans. To deny such inheritance is to deny our faith. But to claim a historic faith also means to claim one that is constantly moving toward God's future, and therefore we must learn to claim our inheritance in such a way that it is a help rather than a hindrance in our march toward the future. In other words, we must learn to reevaluate and reinterpret what has been handed down to us. To do this in the case of Scripture is the primary task of a preacher of liberation.

Many of us who have come to this conclusion find something autobiographic in what Juan Luis Segundo calls the "hermeneutic circle," in which there are four basic moments:

> *Firstly*, there is our way of experiencing reality, which leads us to ideological suspicion. *Secondly* there is the application of our ideological suspicion to the whole ideological superstructure in general and to theology in particular. *Thirdly* there comes a new way of experiencing theological reality that leads us to exegetical suspicion, that is, to the suspicion that the prevailing interpretation of the Bible has not taken important pieces of data into account. *Fourthly* we have our new hermeneutic, that is, our new way of interpreting the fountainhead of our faith (i.e., Scripture) with the new elements at our disposal.[2]

To put these ideas in less terse language, one could say that most of us began with a theological naiveté. We believed, not only that what the Bible said was true, but also that the Bible actually said what our mentors and the tradition before them told us that it said. Then, through a series of episodes, we became conscious of the structures of oppression around and above us, and tried to do something about them. But hardly had we begun to get involved in whatever movement claimed our allegiance, when we were told that what we were doing was unbiblical and antichristian. If ours was a cause of racial justice, we were told that the Bible supported racism. If it was a question of economic justice, we were told that we ought to be concerned about more spiritual matters. If it was a struggle against sexism, we were told that Christian women are to be meek, and that to claim our rights was unchristian pride. At that point, many of our friends and companions saw the need for a choice, and some opted for the movement and abandoned the church, while others did the opposite. Those of us who sought a different alternative were quickly thrust into the second and third steps of Segundo's circle. We became suspicious of the biblical exegesis which was being used against us and came to the conclusion that, like the Reformers of old, we must be willing to read the Bible *de novo*. Thus we came to our "new hermeneutic," and began applying it, eventually to come to the joyful discovery that the Bible was much more on our side than we ever dared hope, and that there were throughout the world a host of others who had gone through parallel struggles and had arrived at similar methodologies and conclusions.

To be able to do liberation theology, a person must first have gone through the painful experience of this circle or of another like it. It does not suffice to come in at the last stage, read up on the methodology of liberation exegesis, study the most significant books, and go out to preach liberation. The facile alacrity with which some have done this is what has given substance to the charge that liberation theology is a fad, for in such cases there is no doubt that there is a high degree of faddism. For such people, liberation theology—which often is no more than liberation vocabulary—is a new insight to be added as an addendum to their list of useful insights.

For the person who has gone through the circle, on the other hand, liberation theology is grounded on a basic suspicion. This is what Segundo calls "ideological suspicion." A black man involved in the struggle against racism has come up against so many instances of hidden racism that he must regard every statement coming out of a predominantly white society as implicitly racist. A woman who is conscious of the prevailing sexism around her must also suspect every statement made by male-dominated theology of being ideologically sexist. From the point of view of those who have not gone through the same painful experiences, such a man and such a woman may seem unduly belligerent and negative. But the truth of the matter is that the experience of going through the hermeneutic circle is so overwhelming that those who have gone through it cannot but refer everything to that experience.

Perhaps an example taken from an entirely different field may be helpful at this point. When Descartes became suspicious of the data of the senses, he came to the conclusion that the only way in which he could attain trustworthy knowledge was to begin by doubting everything. Anything which could should be doubted, not for the sake of doubt, but for the sake of knowledge. To many of his critics, this seemed akin to agnosticism. But Descartes was convinced that this universal doubt was necessary in order to attain certainty. And only those who understood this could be true Cartesians. Likewise, the "ideological suspicion" of the liberation theologian, unbelieving as it may seem from outside, is the only way in which we can be sure that we are doing all that we can to rid biblical interpretation of its traditionally oppressive bias.

Once we have gone through the circle and made it a part of our basic theological outlook, we can once again look at tradition, no longer as that which we have to oppose because it is oppressive, but rather as that which, in our struggle for liberation, we are to reinterpret and reclaim. Tradition then becomes a living reality, in which we discover many kindred spirits whose struggle was akin to ours, but who have been forgotten or obscured by an interpretation which sought to preserve the existing order.

The same is true of the tradition of biblical interpretation. Once we learn to read such interpretation with suspicion, we gain new love and respect, first for the Bible, and then for a tradition of which we too are a part, and which we are helping to shape.

TRADUTTORE TRADITORE

The Italian phrase, *traduttore traditore*—a translator is a traitor—expresses in a nutshell, albeit somewhat mordantly, the dilemma faced by every translator. Languages are not exactly equivalent to each other. A phrase in any language often has nuances and overtones that cannot be expressed in a single phrase in another language. In such cases, the translator is forced to choose between the various shades of meaning and opt for the phrase that seems to convey those shades most faithfully. But anyone who has good command of more than one language, and has ever tried to translate from one to the other, is well aware that the task of translating involves almost constant choice between various alternatives, and that the finished product expresses, not only the views of the original writer, but also the interpretation of the translator.

This is also true of Bible translations. They always reflect, not only the style, but also the biases of the translators. In general, two main approaches have been followed by translators. One has been called the "formal correspondence" approach, and it seeks to translate the biblical text word for word to the point of indicating, by means of different typefaces, when a word had to be added for the sake of clarity or grammar. A typical example of this kind of translation is the King James Version. The second approach, that of "dynamic equivalence," "is concerned first of all with communicating the *content* of the source message in terms meaningful to the receptors. It is thus forced to dispense with *formal* correspondence whenever such correspondence would lead to interference or translationisms that might impede communication."[3] In varying degrees, most "contemporary" translations follow this approach, and a good example is the Good News Bible. Obviously, each of these approaches has its shortcomings. Formal correspondence often leads to translations that are hardly intelligible, but dynamic equivalence gives translators greater latitude in which to exercise their biases. Therefore, preachers of liberation must be particularly aware of the manner in which such biases affect various translations, and if at all possible seek a knowledge of the biblical languages which is sufficiently thorough to be able to judge between various possible translations.

It is obviously impossible to review here the biases that appear in various English translations. But a few examples will give the reader an indication of what some of the problems are.

The use of the words "servant" and "slave" in various English translations of the New Testament would yield abundant material for reflection along these lines. For instance, why is it that most translations (not the King James) refer to Paul as a "servant," and to Onesimus as a "slave," when in fact in Greek both words are the same? Could it not be that, perhaps unconsciously, white translators have been reluctant to have Paul call himself anything as low as a slave? Translators seem to have come to the conclusion that the same word, "doulos," should sometimes be interpreted as "servant," and at other times as "slave," and that they know when to use one, and when the other.

Still dealing with Onesimus and the Epistle to Philemon, we are all well aware of the manner in which that epistle was used in support of slavery, and particularly to argue that runaway slaves ought to be returned to their masters. But what has usually been forgotten is that Paul instructed Philemon to receive Onesimus "no longer as a slave but more than a slave, as a beloved brother" (v. 16 RSV) or "not now as a servant, but above a servant, a brother beloved" (KJ). And, as if to make sure that this was not interpreted in an inner sense, so that Onesimus would continue being a slave with the added appellative of "brother," Paul went on to say that this fraternity was to be "both in the flesh and in the Lord" (KJ and RSV). The result of all this is that the Epistle has traditionally been understood in the sense that Paul simply sent Onesimus back to slavery, with an exhortation to Philemon to call him brother. Thus, the word "slave" was taken literally, and "brother" was taken figuratively, although the text itself gives no basis for such assumptions. But what is even more illuminating is that the New Testament in Today's English Version, *Good News for Modern Man*, perpetuates that interpretation by obscuring the fact that Paul told Philemon to receive Onesimus as a brother "both in the flesh and in the Lord." Compare the import of these two translations of Philemon 16:

. . . no longer as a slave but more than a slave, as a beloved brother, especially to me but how much more to you, both in the flesh and in the Lord. (RSV)

For now he is not just a slave, but much more than a slave: he is a brother in Christ. How much he means to me! And how much more he will mean to you, both as a slave and as a brother in the Lord. (TEV)

The more modern translation, with its effort at dynamic equivalence, has clearly decided that "in the flesh" refers to his slavery, and that Onesimus' brotherhood with Philemon is only "in the Lord."

Another case in point is the choice between "justice" and "righteousness." In the original Greek of the New Testament, these two are the same word. And yet, by consistently translating that word as "righteousness," many translators have left aside the demands of justice, and texts that may well refer to justice are seen as speaking only of a moral rectitude. Take for instance II Corinthians 6:7, "with the weapons of righteousness for the right hand and for the left" and 6:14, "what partnership have righteousness and iniquity?" (RSV), and substitute the word "justice" for "righteousness." Does this not give the text a biting edge that our more common translations seem to miss?

Still on the question of "justice" and "righteousness," it is significant to note that most western European languages have these two options for translating the one Greek word, and that in general those translations done from a position of power—or at least of prestige—seem to prefer "righteousness," and its equivalents, while those done in the midst of persecution, or in other positions of disadvantage, opt for "justice." Again, biblical translation, like biblical interpretation, is not done in a socio-political void.

There are literally hundreds of examples which could be used to show the degree to which sexism has influenced biblical translation. The most common in modern English versions stems from the nature of the English language and its need for an explicit subject for every verb. One cannot simply say "walk," without specifying who is doing the walking. In this respect, Greek is very different from English, for the subject is included in the verb and does not have to be explicitly stated. In the case of the third person, this allows for an indeterminateness which is not possible in English. Take for instance Luke 13:29, where the RSV says: "and men will come from the east and west, . . ." and the KJ: "they shall come from the east and from the west . . ." Why is it that one version says "men" and the other "they"? Simply because the Greek says neither the one nor the other. It uses the third person plural form of the verb and provides no more determinate subject. But, since that cannot be done in English, the translator is left with the need to supply a subject. Significantly, both the RSV and J. B. Phillips choose to use "men," thus simply expressing the commonly held assumption of our society that "man" is the normative form of being human. In this particular case, the TEV is more inclusive: "People will come from the east and the west . . ."

Another example which appears throughout is the use of the male plural form to refer to mixed groups. English has very few words which are gender-specific, like son, daughter, brother, sister, etc., and in any case adjectives and articles have no gender. Thus, if one is speaking about a church in which there are men and women, one is likely to say, for instance: "the dear Christian brothers and sisters." But one could hardly do this in a language such as Greek in which not only "brothers" and "sisters" but also "the," "dear," and "Christian" have genders. The result of such an attempt would be a very awkward phrase: the (masc.) dear (masc.) Christian (masc.) brothers and the (fem.) dear (fem.) Christian (fem.) sisters. In order to avoid this awkward repetition, Greek and other languages with similar characteristics make use of the plural masculine form in order to refer to mixed groups. Thus, for instance, although there is a word for "brothers" and a word for "sisters," when referring to a group of both genders one could easily speak of them as "brothers."[4] Given the nature of the language, this would not automatically exclude "sisters," as the English would.

The result of this is that we often find the New Testament speaking of "brothers," and we may be led to think that the reference is only to males, as it would be in everyday English usage. But the fact is that, given the nature of the Greek language, this may just as well mean "brothers and sisters." And yet, it is interesting to note that all common versions of the Bible translate the Greek plural *adelphoi* as "brothers," and never seem even to consider the possibility that this may be a reference to a group which includes both brothers and sisters.

A very interesting case appears in Romans 16:7. Here two people are called "apostles": Andronicus and Junias. By its form, Junias is clearly a feminine name, but since they are spoken of together, the words for "relatives," "fellow prisoners," and "apostles" are all in the masculine form. This does not mean that Junias is a man, for the masculine form would have been used, no matter whether Paul was speaking of two men or of a man and a woman. All that can be said then regarding gender is that we have here two people, and that the name of one of them appears to be feminine. And yet, the RSV makes the decision for us in translating the passage: "Greet Andronicus and Junias, my kinsmen and my fellow prisoners; they are men of great note among the apostles." At this point one wonders whether the translators were led by grammatical considerations or simply allowed themselves to be influenced by the tacit assumption that no woman could be counted among the apostles.

What all this means is that translations, like all interpretations, have their hidden agendas—sometimes hidden even from the translators themselves. Part of the "ideological suspicion" of those who have gone through the hermeneutic circle must be to question every translation and to seek to check it out with the original before deciding that a particular text is as oppressive as we are told it is. If recourse to the original is not open to us, we must at least compare several different translations. And at this point it may be well to remember that the more a translation relies on the principles of "dynamic equivalence" the more danger there is that the translator's biases will creep in. And paraphrases such as *The Living Bible* are worse than useless, for they reflect the cultural biases of the authors just as much as they reflect the original text.

LECTIONARIES AND COMMENTARIES

Lectionaries are a very useful aid to preaching, for they prevent the preacher from centering on a few favorite passages, books, or themes. All of us have that inclination, and therefore it is helpful to have an outside influence, such as the lectionary, calling our attention to elements in the Gospel message which we may have tended to ignore. The same is true of the church year, which forces us to deal with a variety of themes.

Lectionaries are also helpful in that sometimes they induce us to face up to the relationship between texts that we would otherwise prefer to keep apart. A case in point is Luke 10:25-42 where the parable of the Good Samaritan and the story of Mary and Martha appear back to back. The common interpretation of the parable is that we ought to be concerned about the physical needs of others, above our religious concerns. But then comes the story of Mary and Martha in which Martha, who is making provision for Jesus' physical needs, is told that Mary has chosen the better part. Our normal inclination is to preach about the Good Samaritan when we feel that our congregations are too engrossed in religious matters and not sufficiently involved in the needs of the world, and to preach on Mary and Martha when we fear that the opposite is true. We get away with this by making sure that there are at least a few months between our sermons on these two texts! But what we are really doing in such cases is manipulating Scripture. We know what the two texts say. We diagnose the needs of the congregation. We prescribe the appropriate text in the appropriate dose. We thus seem to have the same control over the Word of God that a physician has over pills and potions. It is obviously impossible totally to avoid this situation. But a good lectionary can serve as a corrective. In the case of Luke 10, for instance, the current lectionary of the Consultation on Church Union, which is the same used, with some variations, by most major Protestant denominations and by Roman Catholics, makes certain that the Good Samaritan and Mary and Martha are dealt with in the same unbroken continuity which they have in Luke 10. In that lectionary, the Good Samaritan is prescribed as the Gospel reading for the eighth Sunday after Pentecost and Mary and Martha for the ninth (year C). But the lectionary also helps us by prescribing, for the preceding and succeeding Sundays, the entire portion of Luke in which these passages appear, thus giving an indication that neither the parable nor the episode of Mary and Martha can be correctly understood apart from the inbreaking of the Kingdom, which is the theme of the earlier part of Luke 10.

But in spite of all these values of a lectionary, preachers of liberation must not forget that lectionaries are a selection which reflects the prevailing tradition of the church, and that therefore they must be seen with the necessary "ideological suspicion," and corrected accordingly.

The first thing a preacher of liberation notices on looking at the current lectionary of the Consultation on Church Union is the sort of passages that are included, and the sort that are omitted. There is no question that, arising out of the period of the struggle for civil rights in the United States, this lectionary shows much more social awareness than its predecessors. But that awareness seems to reflect more the mind-set of liberal theology and liberal politics than that of liberation theology. This is particularly true of the selection of Old Testament texts, which, in very traditional fashion, are most often chosen on the basis of their significance for the Christian religion and its observances, rather than on the basis of their significance in showing God's just and loving dealings with the people. Thus, for instance, although there are many selections from Deuteronomy and Leviticus, these have to do mostly with the prescriptions regarding the passover and the shunning of lepers, and nowhere deal with the much more radical views of these two books, that the land belongs to God and cannot be held in perpetuity by anyone, and that at the time of jubilee there shall be a general release from creditors:

> "The land shall not be sold in perpetuity, for the land is mine; for you are strangers and sojourners with me. And in all the country you possess, you shall grant a redemption of the land.
> "If your brother becomes poor, and sells part of his property, then his next of kin shall come and redeem what his brother has sold. If a man has no one to redeem it, and then himself becomes prosperous and finds sufficient means to redeem it, let him reckon the years since he sold it and pay back the overpayment to the man to whom he sold it; and he shall return to his property. But if he has not sufficient means to get it back for himself, then what he has sold shall remain in the hand of him who bought it until the year of jubilee; in the jubilee it shall be released, and he shall return to his property." (Lev. 25:23-28, RSV)

The text in Deuteronomy 15, which further explains the provision regarding the year of jubilee, is also excluded from this lectionary. (And, let it be said in passing, for those who are wont to quote "the poor you have always with you" as an excuse for not doing anything about poverty, that here Scripture says: "But there will be no poor among you . . . if only you will obey the voice of the Lord your God").

In the same lectionary, there are abundant readings from the prophets. Given the time when this lectionary was compiled, one is not surprised to find in it a number of passages which expound the social doctrine of the prophets. Amos appears three times in a three-year cycle, and in year C, the eighteenth and nineteenth Sunday after Pentecost, there is a good succession of two readings which set forth this prophet's social teachings. But most of the passages from the prophets have been selected because they contain a phrase that has traditionally received a Christological interpretation, and not because they set forth the main thrust of the particular prophet's message. An examination of the selections from Isaiah would bear this out. But, since there are forty-five such passages, it seems best to illustrate our point with the lectionary's use of Micah.

There is only one text from Micah in this lectionary. It is Micah 5:1-5a which is prescribed for the fourth Sunday in Advent (year C), apparently because it includes the words "but you, O Bethlehem Ephrathah, who are little to be among the clans of Judah, from you shall come forth from me one who is to be ruler in Israel, whose origin is from of old, from ancient days." For the Advent season, this is a very appropriate reading. But as the sole text from Micah in a cycle of three years of Bible readings, it does very little to show the radical nature of that prophet's message, how he understood the future which he announced. For that purpose, Micah 4:1-4 would be much more helpful, for it is there that the prophet speaks of a new order of peace—"they shall beat their swords into plowshares, and their spears into pruning hooks"—and justice—"they shall sit every man under his vine and under his fig tree, and none shall make them afraid."

Another omission in several Protestant lectionaries, although understandable, is crucial. The Presbyterian lectionary, for instance, does not include the account of the escape from Egypt, which liberation theologians see as the great instance of God's saving action in the Old Testament. The reason for this is that the lectionary of the Consultation on Church Union includes that text, as has been done for centuries, among those to be read in the vigil of Easter Eve. In adapting that lectionary to their own uses, Protestant denominations that do not have such a vigil simply eliminated those texts, since the lack of awareness of the issues of liberation made it possible for them to leave out this crucial saving act of God.

At other points lectionaries prescribe how we are to interpret the biblical message simply by the way they cut the texts prescribed. Again in the Consultation on Church Union lectionary, the suggested reading for the seventh Sunday after Epiphany (cycle A) is Leviticus 19:1-2, 15-18. Whenever liberation preachers see a text that has been cut up in this fashion, their "ideological suspicion" is aroused. And in this case such suspicion seems to be well founded, for the text to be read tells the congregation of the people of Israel to be holy, but the section omitted puts some teeth on the concrete meaning of holiness:

> "When you reap the harvest of your land, you shall not reap your field to its very border, neither shall you gather the gleanings after your harvest. And you shall not strip your vineyard bare; . . . you shall leave them for the poor and for the sojourner: I am the Lord Your God.
> "You shall not steal, nor deal falsely, nor lie to one another. And you shall not swear by my name falsely, and so profane the name of your God: I am the Lord.
> "You shall not oppress your neighbor or rob him. The wages of a hired servant shall not remain with you all night until the morning. You shall not curse the deaf or put a stumbling block before the blind, but you shall fear your God: I am the Lord." (Lev. 19:9-13, RSV)

Another place at which some "ideologically suspicious" cropping has been done is in the New Testament passages dealing with the relationship between wives and husbands, fathers and children, and masters and slaves. The longest and best known of these passages is Ephesians 5:21–6:9. The text deals with the relationships between three sets of powerful and powerless people: husbands and wives, fathers and children, and masters and slaves. Yet the lectionary ends the reading at the end of chapter 5, thus omitting the sections on fathers and children, and on masters and slaves. This seems to make sense, since the break comes at the end of a chapter, and in any case we no longer have slavery. But what is avoided by cutting the text at this point is being forced to see the connection between the issue of slavery and that of the submission of wives. If we read the whole text, we must be honest and say that whatever we do about what is said there regarding slavery, we must also do about husbands and wives. By reading only the section in chapter 5, we are able to deal with the question of relations between spouses as if those were fixed forever, while the matter of slavery was a passing episode in human history.

In the case of Ephesians, this pruning of the text could be excused on the grounds that it comes at the end of a chapter—although no one would claim that the division into chapters and verses is part of the inspired canon. But when we look at the way the lectionary deals with the parallel text in Colossians, our suspicion is justified, for there again the text is cut before coming to the issue of slavery, and this is done in the middle of a paragraph.

The third text in which such "household legislation" appears in the New Testament has also been cropped in a strange way. The entire passage is I Peter 2:18–3:7. But what the lectionary prescribes is only the middle of it, 2:19-22. What thus takes place is that the entire congregation hears out of context words which were originally addressed to slaves!

A final example of interesting cropping has to do with the slaughter of the innocents. The lectionary of the Consultation on Church Union sets as the Gospel lesson for the first Sunday after Christmas, Matthew 2:13-15, 19-23. When we look to see what has been omitted, we discover that it is the slaughter of the innocents. Further inquiry yields some interesting observations. The first of these is that the historical reason why this text appears in this place is that the Roman Church has traditionally celebrated the day of the Holy Innocents on December 28, and that therefore readings having to do with the slaughter of the infants, and with the flight into Egypt, were placed around that date. But a second observation is that this

breaks the sequence of the Gospel narrative, for it places the lessons
having to do with the arrival of the magi on January 6, long after both
the slaughter of the children and the flight into Egypt. Were that the
real sequence, the magi would have found an empty stable!

When we apply our ideologically suspicious methodology to all
this, we discover that the present order of readings breaks the
connection between the actions of the magi and their consequences.
The Gospel text, read in sequence, shows that both the slaughter of
the innocents and the flight into Egypt are the direct result of the
magi's actions. But the magi have become objects of veneration in
the church. As signs of the coming of the Gospel to the Gentiles,
they are our forerunners. In popular tradition, they are rich and wise
men (the word *magus* does not necessarily mean a "wise" person, as
we understand wisdom today, but rather an astrologer, diviner, and
interpreter of dreams). We even take them to be kings, although
again, there is nothing in the text that says they were. Such powerful,
rich, and wise men cannot make the stupid blunder of warning
Herod about the birth of Jesus, and thus causing the flight into Egypt
and the slaughter of the innocents. Therefore, the church calendar,
and the lectionaries based on it, must hide the fact that they
did—although the older Presbyterian lectionary did have the reading
of the flight into Egypt and the slaughter of the innocents on the
evening of Epiphany, thus showing the connection between them
and the actions of the magi. And yet, this blunder of the supposedly
wise and religious, hidden by the wise and religious who have
developed the church year, is crystal clear to the poor in Nicaragua,
as we shall see later.

In conclusion, lectionaries, being a part of the tradition of the
church, reflect that tradition, in both its positive and its negative
features. Therefore, the liberation preacher's attitude toward them
should be the same as toward Christian tradition in general. We
accept them as part of the continuing history of which we also are a
part. We value what they have to teach us regarding the amplitude
of the biblical message. Yet we do not submit to them blindly, but
rather approach them with the same "ideological suspicion" with
which we approach the entirety of Christian tradition and
theology.

We have dwelt at length on lectionaries, and particularly on that suggested by the Consultation on Church Union, because they are widely used by many churches and thus provide us with the opportunity to show the hidden hand of tradition in an instrument of biblical interpretation which has fairly general currency. But we could also have done the same with some of the other instruments of biblical interpretation.

Commentaries, for instance, are not ideologically neutral. Most of them take for granted that the best and only way to understand the Bible is through meticulous and scholarly study of words, historical data, form criticism, etc. It is true that without such tools we run the risk of clearly false interpretations. But it is also true that all these tools do not suffice for a true understanding of the biblical message. At this point many will agree and point out that true understanding also requires piety, that it is impossible to understand the biblical message as an outsider, as someone who is not committed to it. And that is precisely the point. But we must hasten to add that such piety, which is absolutely necessary in order to understand the Bible, must be *biblical* piety. It cannot be what our culture, and many of our churches after it, deem to be piety. It must be the piety which consists in being part of the people of God, marching after the promised Kingdom of peace and justice. In other words, it must be piety which lives in symbiosis with what liberation theologians call "praxis."

The problem, then, with most of the current commentaries is that they are written from a perspective that takes for granted that scholarly knowledge, or that plus simple religiosity, suffice to understand the Bible. They thus perpetuate the unbiblical notion that the cultured, the wise, and the secure have an edge when it comes to understanding the will of God, whereas the Bible repeatedly states that the first shall be last, that Jesus came to bring "good news to the poor," that things hidden from the wise have been revealed to babes, and in general that if any have an edge on understanding what God is all about it is the outcast, the poor, the despised, and the oppressed. No amount of scholarly inquiry can erase the handicap of the respectable and respected Bible commentator.

Again, this does not mean that the preacher of liberation should not use commentaries. Without them, we could easily miss the meaning of many words, the grammatical structure of passages, parallel texts that illumine their meaning, etc. But it does mean that we should approach biblical commentaries, no matter how seemingly objective, with the same "ideological suspicion" with which we approach the entirety of the Christian tradition and theology. As a normal practice, it may be well to postpone the reading of commentaries until, through the use of some of the methods outlined elsewhere in this book, we come to the point where we hear what we believe to be God's word in the text for our concrete situation and struggle. After that, commentaries will prove useful instruments whereby to make certain that we have not completely misinterpreted the text or to discover nuances and connections which we had not noticed before.

The principle of "ideological suspicion" holds true as we use any of the other tools of academic theological inquiry or of sermon preparation, such as theological treatises, monographic studies about the Bible, famous sermons, etc. All of these may be helpful; but the first thing a preacher of liberation asks is, what are the oppressive biases which find subtle expression in this writing? What view of reality and of God's purposes does this writing espouse, perhaps without even being aware of it?

A case in point would be the liberation preacher's approach to the collection of sermons which serves as a companion to the series of which this book is a part, *The Twentieth Century Pulpit.*[5] A rapid glance at the list of contributors shows that they are all male, and that almost all of them are white—it would have been impossible to exclude Martin Luther King, Jr. from such a collection. That already says something to the ideologically suspicious about where the editor believes significant preaching is taking place. In reading this book, one will undoubtedly find a great deal that is of value. There is, for instance, Karl Barth's Ascension Day sermon, "Look up to Him!" But one will also be on guard lest one may surreptitiously come to accept the implied assumption that white, North-Atlantic males are indeed today's best exponents of the biblical message. One can then admire these preachers' elegance of style, imaginative flair and even—though unfortunately in not too many cases—faithful exposition of Scripture. But one can do this without losing sight of the more radically biblical preaching that is taking place in political prisons in Latin America, in black churches in the United States, and in the many situations of conflict where, today, God is bringing release to the captives and setting at liberty those who are oppressed.

III. THE FORGOTTEN INTERPRETERS

In the previous chapter, we gave some examples of the difficulties that stand in the way of our listening anew to the biblical text. Most of these are hidden and therefore difficult to overcome. But in any case, the present chapter and the next will give some examples of the ways in which a preacher of liberation can seek to hear the word of the Bible in a new and liberating way.

THE END OF THE LONE-RANGER BIBLE STUDY

For too long there has been in Protestant circles an excessive emphasis on private Bible study. There is no doubt that such study is necessary. There is no point in ten people jointly looking up a word in a Hebrew lexicon. When one adds to this the devotional dimension, there is also no doubt that there is an important place in the Christian life for private devotions, and that these ought to be centered on the study of the Bible. But the problem comes when we seem to say that private Bible study is somehow better or deeper or more meaningful than corporate study. To make matters worse, in the services of some of our churches—often those that pride themselves on being most "biblical"—very little attention is paid to the Bible. In some cases, even the sermon, rather than attempting to put us under the scrutiny and the mercy of the Word of God, uses the biblical text as a pretext, as a jumping off point from which to go far afield. Take for instance the sermon "Ride the Wild Horses!" in *The Twentieth Century Pulpit*. Its text is taken from James 3:3: "If we put bits into the mouths of horses to make them obey us, we guide their whole bodies." The preacher then begins by saying: "The wild horses we have to deal with are our instincts—the untamed impulses of human nature." This may be true, and all the rest of the sermon may be true. But when we look at the text in James, we see that the reference is not to instincts in general, but to the unbridled tongue, and particularly to the unbridled tongue of those who claim to be teachers:

> Let not many of you become teachers, my brethren, for you know that we who teach shall be judged with greater strictness. For we all make many mistakes, and if any one makes no mistakes in what he says he is a perfect man, able to bridle the whole body also. If we put bits into the mouths of horses that they may obey us, we guide their whole bodies. Look at the ships also; though they are so great and are driven by strong winds, they are guided by a very small rudder wherever the will of the pilot directs. So the tongue is a little member and boasts of great things. How great a forest is set ablaze by a small fire! (James 3:1-5, RSV)

Such is the theme of the passage from which the author of this otherwise eloquent sermon takes his text. But it is to be feared that, precisely because the text has been taken out of context and used simply as a starting point for a discussion on the Christian attitude toward the instincts and passions, this sermon may verge on being an example of precisely the use of the tongue that so worried the author of the epistle!

Things were very different in the early church. Since there was no printing press, copies of Scripture were not available for all to have at home, and therefore when the congregation gathered a great deal of time was spent reading the Scriptures—at first the Old Testament, to which soon were added the "memoirs of the apostles" (gospels) and the epistles. The sermon was expected to be an exposition of Scripture.

It may be argued that the invention of the printing press, and the resultant fact that all Christians can read their Bibles at home, has changed this situation, and that therefore there is little or no need for that sort of corporate Bible study. But the problem is that most of the Bible was written to be read, not in private, but in public, often within the context of corporate worship. Just as it is not the same to read a sermon as it is to hear it preached, it is not the same to read the Bible in private as it is to read it and hear it being read in the midst of the people of God. The Lone-Ranger student of the Bible loses a great deal that cannot be regained by any amount of study or private devotion.

But the Lone Ranger himself did not roam the West alone. He had Tonto with him. Tonto, whose name means "dimwit," as any Hispanic in the southwest would know. Tonto, who hardly ever spoke, except for an occasional, either enigmatic or meaningless, "kemo sabe." And in spite of this the white hero was called "lone," because his Indian companion, who repeatedly saved his life, simply did not count. He did not count for two reasons: first, he was seen as a projection of his white leader; second, the Lone Ranger never seemed to take the time to listen to him.

There is then a type of "Lone-Ranger" Bible study which, although not necessarily done in private, is done in the same sort of almost meaningless company which Tonto provided for the hero. This happens when our biblical interpretation fails to be challenged by others, either because they share our own perspective, or because, since they differ from us, we classify them as "Tontos" whose perspectives we need not take into account.

The ideologically suspicious liberation preacher soon comes to the realization that, given the social structure of our denominations and of our housing patterns, it is very difficult to avoid the Lone-Ranger Bible study. We may try to have more corporate study of the Bible, and there is certainly something to be gained from doing so, but it is still difficult to provide for the various perspectives which would allow us to see the Bible in a different light.

Even within the social uniformity and racial monochrome of most of our churches, there is a degree of diversity which could be helpful. There are, for instance, people of different ages and genders. And yet, even here there is a tendency to segregate our Bible study by age and by gender! Granted that there is a place for a graded Sunday school and for women's circles of Bible study, do we not lose something of the enrichment that we could be to each other when most or all our study of the Bible is done in such settings? If it is true of the preaching of the Kingdom that God has "hidden these things from the wise and understanding and revealed them to babes" (Luke 10:21), do not adults cheat themselves out of the opportunity for deeper insight into the will of God when they fail to provide for Bible study that cuts across age gaps? And, if it is true that those who are oppressed and whom society counts as nothing go first into the kingdom of God, do not young adults miss an opportunity to see the work of God when they put the aged "out to pasture" and do not give them an opportunity to show them, through constant interaction in love, what the Bible says from the perspective of those who once were powerful and respected, but now often find themselves merely tolerated?

Something similar is true in the case of women. The difference between their experience and that of men should be a significant factor in the study of the Bible, especially since traditionally most biblical commentary and exegesis has been done from a male perspective. It is common for male preachers to try to guess what women will find significant, or how they will react to a certain text. And usually they fail miserably! An easy experiment, which may serve to show this, is to ask a group of men to list the five passages in the Bible that they believe will be most significant for women, and then to ask a group of women to list the five passages that they themselves have found most significant in their Christian lives. Chances are that there will be very little overlapping between the two lists. Men will usually choose those passages that speak about women, whereas women will list those that speak of strength in the midst of difficulty or of confidence when there is cause for despair. What this shows is that, quite unconsciously, men tend to believe that the Bible is addressed to them, for they are the typical, normative human beings, and that only those passages which speak of females will be of significance to women. It often comes as a shock to discover, not only that these are not the passages that the women list, but also that their interpretation of the passages that they do choose shows valuable insights derived from their experience as females.

When it comes to questions of class, race, and culture, the average North American white church finds it much more difficult to overcome the Lone-Ranger syndrome. They are willing to see their sisters and brothers of other groups as fellow travelers in the Christian life, and are even willing to help them along. But they still will tend to see them as "Tontos" whose contribution to the understanding of the Christian message will be no more than a grunt or an occasional "kemo sabe." Even where there is an interest in hearing what these people have to say, the social and racial composition of most white churches makes it very difficult. In order to be able to listen to what the supposed "Tontos" are saying and to the way they experience and interpret the message of the Bible, it is necessary to have a close association with them, to share in their experience, in a way and to a degree that very few in the white community are willing to risk.

There is a positive side to this, for were the white Christian community suddenly to begin showing greater interest in what the traditionally silent have to say, that interest would smack of mere curiosity, just as the interest in helping the poor and downtrodden smacks of paternalism. It is for this reason that many liberation theologians hesitate to speak to predominantly white, North American audiences. They fear that their insights, gained through the painful process of the hermeneutic circle, will be turned into one more consumer item, that they will become one more fad in the North American theological scene so given to fads. And their fears are more than justified.

What then of the sincere, white, male preacher who believes that there are valuable insights in liberation theology and wishes to pursue them to make them his own and to lead his congregation in appropriating them and living them out? For such a person, there is only one way: the pain and struggle of the hermeneutic circle. He cannot live out of another's experience of oppression. He must discover how the system that oppresses the black, the Hispanic, the native American, and the woman, also oppresses him. He must come to see for himself how much of the theology he has been taught serves to bolster that system of oppression. He must develop the ideological suspicion without which there is no liberation theology. He must begin to work for his own liberation. He must do his theology out of that struggle. And then he will really be able to look at the theology of liberation of other groups, and to learn from it.

Once the liberation preacher comes to this point, there are a number of resources available. These are helpful, both for the white male preacher who must do groundwork on the meaning of his own liberation, and for those preachers who belong to various movements of liberation, but who may gain insight from other movements or other experiences. In the next two sections of this chapter, we shall deal with some of those resources.

RESOURCES FROM CHRISTIAN TRADITION

It may seem odd to begin a discussion on a liberation reading of Scripture and theology by discussing the resources of Christian tradition. Indeed, many of those who are involved in the various movements of liberation feel that Christian tradition has been so oppressive that it must be discarded altogether. Others, mostly those who come out of a background of liberal theology, have been taught that the past is a burden of which they must rid themselves, and that what must be done is to interpret Christianity in a "modern" way, more adapted to our present circumstances.

It is true that a great deal of Christian tradition has been oppressive. It is also true that, if the Word of God is to be relevant, it must be relevant *today*, and that the very notion of history, so central to a liberation understanding of the gospel, implies that today's preaching will not be the same as yesterday's. But in spite of all this, there is still a great deal of Christian tradition that must be recovered.

That recovery is a difficult task, for from a very early date the process began by which those elements of the tradition that could not be assimilated into the status quo were suppressed or ignored. We have already referred to Eusebius' attempt to show that the persecutions were little more than a grave misunderstanding on the part of the Roman Empire. More recent historians have also read history in a similar manner. For instance, treatises on the ethics of the early church deal almost exclusively with sexual mores, lying, homicide, and so forth, but fail to take into account the astonishing teachings of early Christian writers regarding property, the use and distribution of wealth, and the like. The reason for this is that the definition of what are "ethical" questions has been narrowed in our capitalist society, precisely so as not to include issues such as whether private property is morally correct, or what are the rights of the poor. On the basis of such a definition, historians of Christian ethics tend to ignore the very radical things that have been said in earlier centuries of Christian history and thus give us the impression that today's radical questioning of the rights of property, for instance, is a new phenomenon, about which Christian tradition has little to say.

The ideologically suspicious preacher of liberation is not quick to accept such a verdict, but rather asks a further question: Is the history of Christian ethics a faithful rendering of what ancient Christians actually taught, or is it rather one more case in which the interests of the powerful are being served by what seems to be impartial scholarship? Even before examining the evidence, such an ideologically suspicious person will remember that the early church was not generally composed of rich and powerful people, and will therefore expect to find a different perspective than that which seems to pervade Christian teaching in later times.

Although this is not the only issue with which various theologies of liberation deal, let us for the moment center our attention on economic matters, and we may be surprised by what we shall find in early Christian writings. On this score, the picture that most of us have is that of a primitive church that had all things in common, discovered that such a system did not work, and promptly forgot it, together with any attempt to reorder or critique the existing economic system. But, although it is true that soon the church began having some rich folk in its midst, and therefore began to mollify some of Jesus' strictures against the rich, it is also true that for centuries it kept alive an understanding of God's will that there should be neither rich nor needy, but that all should have that which was necessary for their sustenance, and that some of its leaders had very harsh words to say about the prevailing economic system and those who profited from it.

Ignatius of Antioch, who wrote seven letters early in the second century while on his way to martyrdom, has been correctly depicted as a zealous defender of orthodoxy. But what most scholars have failed to note is that to him orthodoxy was not only a matter of proper doctrine, but also a matter of right relationship to those in need:

> As to those who profess teachings that have nothing to do with the grace of Jesus Christ . . . you must come to a full realization that those doctrines are completely opposed to the mind of God, for they care nothing about love, they care not for the widow and the orphan, they care not for the hard pressed, nor do they care who is in chains or free, or who is hungry or thirsty.[1]

And a few decades later, Hermas wrote that those who are in need live anxious and tormented lives to the point that some of them are driven to commit homicide, and that any Christian who knows of a person in dire need and fails to respond to that situation may be guilty of homicide.[2]

On the other hand, already at the time of Hermas the rich were joining the church in increasing numbers, and there were those who sought to make it easier for them. Thus, for instance, Clement of Alexandria, in his treatise, *Who Is the Rich to Be Saved?* turned what Jesus had to say to the rich ruler into an allegory and said that what mattered was not the riches themselves, but one's attachment to them. If one had riches, but one loved God above them, they would be no obstacle to salvation, but rather a help, for one could then perform greater works of charity.

The question of property and its use, however, became crucial after the conversion of Constantine. Many who flocked to the church were rich. Most church leaders simply accepted such people and were all too glad to have them add part of their wealth and prestige to the church. But there were many others who, while not absolutely refusing to receive the rich, felt that they must insist on the old Christian teachings regarding riches and the responsibility of those who had more than they needed toward those others who were in want. Most of the great "fathers" of the church held economic views which would be considered quite radical in our day.

Ambrose of Milan, for instance, says that "the earth has been created in common for all, rich and poor. Why do you [the rich] claim for yourselves the right to own the land?"[3] And in another place he says that "God created all things to be the common food, and the land to be the common possession of all. Thus, nature begat the common right, and usurpation begat the private."[4] The result of this is that, when you give to the needy, "you do not give to the poor what is yours, but rather return what is theirs."[5] The reason why the birds of the air do not go hungry is that they do not claim anything in particular for each of them, but rather share equally the bounty of God.[6] But a few rich claim everything for themselves, "not only the land, but the sky, the air, the sea,"[7]—and here one is reminded of today's quip that solar energy will be developed when someone invents a way to hang a meter on the sun—with the result that "every day are the needy murdered."[8]

These views were shared by many of the great Christian leaders of the fourth and fifth century. Among them, Basil the Great says to the rich: "The bread that you hoard belongs to the hungry. The cloak that you keep in your chests belongs to the naked. The shoes that rot in your house belong to the unshod."[9] And therefore, anyone who can do something for the needy and refuses to do so is justly condemned as a homicide.[10] But Basil goes even farther than Ambrose in attacking the wanton growth of capital: "The beasts become fertile when they are young, but quickly cease to be so. But capital produces interest from the very beginning, and this in turn multiplies unto infinity. All that grows ceases to do so when it reaches its normal size. But the money of the greedy never stops growing."[11] And this progression of power is ever accelerating:

> . . . Those who attain a certain level of power use those whom they have already enslaved in order to gain more strength to commit ever greater iniquities, and by using them they enslave those who were still free. Then their greater power becomes a new weapon for evil. And as a result those whom they first injured now have no other option but to help them, and thus collaborate in the evil and iniquity committed against the others.[12]

A host of other witnesses could be adduced to show the radicality of the economic doctrine of those great church leaders. Jerome agrees with the common saying that those who are rich are such either through their own injustice or through that of those whose property they have inherited.[13] Zeno of Verona says that greed is the reason why some people's granaries are full, while others' stomachs are empty. And he goes on to comment that, whereas that which has been taken by force can sometimes be recovered, that which has been taken under the shade of the law can never be recovered.[14] Augustine,[15] Lactantius,[16] Cyril,[17] and Gregory the Great[18] are all in agreement that private property is not of God, that it is the reason why many are in want, and also the root of discord and war.

Since this is a book on preaching, it may be well to conclude this long series of authorities by looking at the sermons of the most renowned of the preachers of antiquity, St. John Chrysostom—"the goldenmouthed." Following the long established tradition to which we have already referred, Chrysostom agrees that iniquity is the only possible source of great riches, for if it is not the very person who is opulent that has committed the necessary iniquities, it must have been that person's ancestors.[19] Since the earth is the Lord's, and the fulness thereof, nothing is to be held by any as privately owned.[20] The rich are not really such, for what they have belongs to others.[21] Anything that one might have, even though legitimately earned, in truth belongs to the poor.[22] And the unjust distribution of wealth increases as time goes by, for all are drawn into the whirlwind of greed, with each trying to outdo those who have gone on before.[23] The rich try to glorify themselves by building opulent palaces, but after their death passersby who never knew them say, "How many tears must that house have cost! How many widows must have suffered injustice, and laborers cheated out of their wages!"[24] Therefore, the result of the vainglory of the rich is exactly the opposite of what they had sought, for even after their death they are cursed, and even by those who never knew them. Finally, it is significant that, commenting on Matthew 25, Chrysostom points out that the judge does not condemn those on his left "because you fornicated, because you committed adultery, because you stole, because you gave false witness or committed perjury. All of these sins are obviously evil, but not as great as callousness and lack of humanity."[25]

Such were the teachings of the first centuries regarding property, riches, and the economic order. And although never again as prevalent as at that time, such teachings were never entirely abandoned.[26]

So far we have dealt only with the question of riches and of the existing economic order. But it is well known that, on such matters as slavery, the church remained silent for centuries. At least, so have we been led to believe. However, when we begin studying the tradition on our own, without the filtering process that has become so common, we find startling cases of opposition to slavery, such as the following words of Gregory of Nyssa, addressed to a slaveowner:

> "I have bought slaves, male and female." Pray tell, at what price? What have you found among all the creatures that is worth as much as human nature? How much money is the mind worth? How many oboli do you consider the image of God to be worth? How many staters did you pay in order to walk away with this creature of God? "Let us make man in our own image and likeness," said God. Tell me, then, who dares buy, who dares sell, the one that is the image of God, who is to rule over the earth, who received from God as an heir all that there is upon the earth? Such power belongs only to God. And I am inclined to say that not even to God. [27]

And yet, we were told that it took Christians centuries to come to the conclusion that slavery was against the divine will, when what in fact did happen was that voices such as that of Gregory and Chrysostom were drowned by those in the church who catered to the powerful.

Surely when it comes to the issues of women and their place in society the situation must be different. And indeed it is, for most of the writings that we have come from males—many of them male ascetics who felt threatened by the very existence of women. But even in this case one occasionally finds startling words, such as the following, addressed by Cyprian to a consecrated virgin in the church:

> "I will multiply," says God to the woman, "thy sorrows and thy groanings; and in sorrow shalt thou bring forth children, and thy desire shall be to thy husband, and he shall rule over thee." You are free from this sentence. You do not fear the sorrows and the groans of women. You have no fear of child-bearing; nor is your husband Lord over you; but your Lord and Head is Christ, after the likeness and in place of man; with that of men your lot and your condition is equal. [28]

In conclusion, although there is no doubt that a great deal of Christian tradition has been oppressive, it is also true that there has been a filtering of the tradition, so that what we now perceive is a distorted view of the past of the church. Thus, the liberation preacher will carry the principle of ideological suspicion a step further and refuse to take for granted that when we are told that there is nothing useful in the church's past such a statement is true. It may well be that the seemingly sympathetic statement is simply an expression of the way tradition appears after it has been filtered by the interests of the powerful. It may well be that a rereading of documents from the Christian past, particularly those produced by people who were persecuted, maligned, or otherwise opposed by the powerful, will yield fresh insights into the meaning of Scripture when read, so to speak, from below.

CONTEMPORARY RESOURCES

In order to avoid the Lone-Ranger syndrome, the preacher of liberation may begin to establish a dialogue with earlier Christian tradition. But this is a life-long task, and in any case it is difficult to establish dialogue with those who are long dead. Fortunately, there are other resources which lie much closer to us. These are the resources of those who are engaged in struggles similar to ours. There we find support in the adventure of reading Scripture anew, and even a great deal of insight which we can apply almost immediately.

For those of us who are members of one of the groups where there already exists a liberation movement and a liberation theology—blacks, Hispanics, women, Third World people, etc.—there is no need to be told to make use of those resources which come from our own movement. Black preachers of liberation will be familiar with the writings of James Cone, and Latin Americans will have read Gustavo Gutierrez' and Juan Luis Segundo's books. What we may need to be told is to remember the resources coming from other movements.

This is important, for these various movements will necessarily clash. Blacks in the United States resent white women entering the labor market and taking the lower paying jobs that used to be theirs.

They will also resent the growing attention which the Hispanic minority is receiving in the media. All oppressed groups in the United States will find their situation worsened, at least at first, by any Third World revolution which stops some of the flow of wealth to the United States. Furthermore, those who are in power will foster such conflicts between various oppressed groups. Therefore, there is a tendency for each movement to look after itself—and in a certain way they must, for no one else will.

But we must remember that we are not struggling only against a particular person or group that oppresses us. We are struggling against a system that prevents the fulfillment of God's purposes for all human creatures. Therefore, we know that there is a connection between racism, classism, colonialism, and sexism. Each of our groups may be attacking the apocalyptic beast from a different angle, and the beast may defend itself by setting us against each other. But we know that the beast is only one, and that the victory won by the Lamb and promised to us is also one.

For these reasons, preachers of liberation who are already involved in a particular movement must not eschew those resources which come from other movements. There they will come to a deeper understanding of the nature of the oppression against which we struggle and will also gain insights into the meaning of the gospel message which they could not have gained from their own group.

Furthermore, as has already been pointed out, most of us stand on different sides of the various liberation movements. A Hispanic male may be part of the oppressed minority, but as a male he must also become aware of the oppression of women, both in his culture and in others. A white North American woman may be involved in the liberation of women, and as such have a consciousness of the oppression of women. But from the point of view of liberation from colonialism, she is part of the society of over-consumption which so oppresses the Third World. Therefore, as each of us approaches the resources available from other movements, we must use our own experience of oppression and our own having gone through the hermeneutic circle, to understand what those other movements have to say.

These resources are also valuable for the white male preacher of liberation. The main problem which such a preacher will encounter is that his movement is practically nonexistent. He will have to create his own consciousness-raising and support groups. He will have to start almost "from scratch" in his task of reading the Bible anew. It is at this point that the resources of other movements which are farther along may be valuable. Obviously, such a preacher will have to avoid the temptations of mere curiosity and the trap of paternalism. And, once again, the only way to avoid those temptations and that trap is to be involved in his own struggle for liberation and to learn to live with the ideological suspicion which is born out of such a struggle.

What has just been said about male white preachers also holds true for predominantly white, middle-class congregations. Obviously, the presence of women in such congregations will give them more direct access into the experience and the theology of an existing movement. But with regard to issues of race, class, and the international order, such a congregation must beware of the same temptations and the same trap. It too must come to the conclusion that it suffers its own oppression, that it must oppose the system, not only "out there" in some distant country, but also at home, where it impinges on our lives through housing, marketing, and advertising practices, through the manipulation of government by large corporations, and in dozens of insidious ways. It must then develop its own ideological suspicion and begin asking some very hard questions, before it will really be able to make proper use of the resources offered by the various groups and movements of oppressed people.

Having come to this consciousness, we can turn to the resources offered by various groups. Obviously, this is not the place to offer an exhaustive introduction to such resources, whose number is rapidly increasing. What we shall attempt will be simply to offer some examples, in order to show what words of biblical and theological insight are coming from those whom the Lone Rangers take to be no more than dimwitted Tontos.

Unfortunately, the insights of the poor and the oppressed seldom reach printed form. But we have a startling exception in Ernesto Cardenal's *The Gospel in Solentiname*. [29] Cardenal is a mystic and a poet, a priest and a political activist, who founded the lay monastery of Our Lady of Solentiname on an island in a lake in Nicaragua. On Sundays, after the reading of the Gospel, Cardenal encouraged the people of the islands—most of them fishermen and their wives, with an occasional student back home for the weekend—to discuss the lesson for the day. The book is simply the transcribed tapes of those conversations. The North American reader may be surprised —perhaps even shocked—by the radical political views of the group and by the way their views are related to the gospel. This alone may serve as a corrective to our tendency to read the Bible in purely "religious" terms. But there is also in the comments of many of these uneducated people an insight into the meaning of various texts, an ability to see what scholarly commentators hardly ever note, which seems to prove the contention that the poor and the oppressed have an edge when it comes to understanding the meaning of the Bible.

In discussing the Annunciation, for instance (Luke 1:26-36), these poor people seem to be much more aware of what is going on than are most of our better educated congregations:

> Someone said: "That angel was being subversive just by announcing that. It's as though someone in Somoza's Nicaragua was announcing a liberator. . . ." And another added: "And Mary joins the ranks of the subversives, too, just by receiving that message. I suppose that by doing that she probably felt herself entering into a kind of underground. The birth of the liberator had to be kept secret. It would be known only by the most trusted and a few of the poor people around there, villagers."[30]

And at the end of the conversation a certain Alejandro shows a profound understanding of the relationship between obedience, love, and risk: "It seems to me that here we should admire above all her [Mary's] obedience. And so we should be ready to obey too. This obedience is revolutionary, because it's obedience to love. Obedience to love is very revolutionary, because it commands us to disobey everything else."[31]

We have already referred to the political blunder of the magi as they asked around in Jerusalem where was the new king of the Jews that had been born. This point, usually missed by commentators, did not escape the sagacity of these poor and uneducated

Nicaraguans, and one of them remarked that "it would be like someone going to Somoza now to ask him where's the man who's going to liberate Nicaragua."[32]

A final example comes from a discussion of the Wedding at Cana (John 2:1-12). We are so used to reading the Bible as a religious document, and so sure of what is proper within the field of religion and what is not, that we miss a great deal of what the Bible has to say against sanctimonious religiosity. But these fisherfolk in Managua do not react in the same way. They realize that what is going on is a big party. One of them comments, after been told how much water Jesus turned into wine: "Six hundred quarts. They really got plastered." Another observes "isn't it interesting that Jesus gets himself involved for a party? His hour will come sooner because he gave wine at a party. It wasn't for anything more serious." But the most surprising comment is made by Pablo Hurtado, who does not speak too often: "If all the water they had for purifying themselves turned into wine on them, now how were they going to perform their ceremonies? I'm sure some of them must have asked him: 'Master, and now how do I purify myself?' And he must have answered them: 'The orders are to have a drink.' "[33]

To our minds, trained to believe about Jesus only that which is proper, this seems sacrilegious. But, does it not come closer than most of our interpretations to the spirit of the Master's teachings and of his repeated disapproval of the religious folk of his time?

The same sort of insight comes from the women's movement. Joanna Dewey, after asserting that we must "read the Bible afresh,"[34] proceeds to a study of the beginning of the book of Exodus from which she draws unexpected, but well substantiated conclusions:

> Certainly in both the story about the midwives and the story of the women's rescue of the baby, the women are acting independently and not as adjuncts of men.
> In both stories the actions of the women are actions of disobedience to the authority of Pharaoh. . . . And in both stories the disobedience results in deliverance: The disobedience of the midwives saves the Hebrew people; the disobedience of the mother, sister, and Pharaoh's daughter saves Moses. . . .
> And if God was later acting through Moses to deliver the people, then

God first of all acted through these women to deliver the people. Women as well as men are God's agents of salvation and, in the story of the exodus, God's first agents. [35]

When one reads the biblical account, one is forced to conclude that she is right. And yet, how many of us have heard sermons stating this fact? By bringing their own experience to bear on the reading of the texts, Professor Dewey and other women are offering the entire church new insights into the biblical message.

Some of these insights have to do with the impact of Jesus' teaching on the commonly accepted views regarding women. Those women who have become conscious of the manner in which they are usually stereotyped object to the prevalent view that a woman is to be defined above all else in her roles as mother and wife. They do not object to those options, nor do they seek to demean their values, just as no normal male would object to the options and the values of being a husband and a father. What they reject is the notion that, while such roles are not all that a man is expected to be, women are often seen only as real, potential, or frustrated wives and mothers. This obviously serves to keep women at home in their subservient roles, and to prevent them from competing with men in other fields of endeavor. As in other such cases, the traditional interpretation of the Bible leads one to believe that the women who object to such stereotyping will find no support in it. But exactly the opposite is shown by women such as Rachel Conrad Wahlberg, who focuses her attention on two well-known passages whose import for these issues usually goes unnoticed.

The first of these is Luke 11:27-28: "As he said this, a woman in the crowd raised her voice and said to him, 'Blessed is the womb that bore you, and the breasts that you sucked!' But he said, 'Blessed rather are those who hear the word of God and keep it!' " (RSV).

Most traditional interpretation centers on the fact that Jesus corrected the woman. Others use this text as an argument against the excessive veneration of Mary. But what only a woman could feel and point out is that here Jesus is rejecting the stereotype of a woman as first of all a reproductive being. This is what Rachel Conrad Wahlberg points out:

Subsequent centuries have been so accepting of the stereotyped woman that they have not noticed what Jesus said. Religious interpreters have not known what to do with this radical rejection by Jesus of the uterus image. Does he mean to put down the idea of woman as child-bearer? Is he demeaning her function as a fetus-carrier and a baby-suckler?

Remember that only if a woman had children, and preferably boys, was she honored. If she were "barren" she was regarded as one to be pitied. Actually her status in that society was based on the uterus image. Her worth *was* in her procreativeness.

It is mind-blowing to realize that Jesus was actually rejecting this commonly accepted justification for the existence of woman. If not a child-bearer, what was woman? Jesus is saying: *She is one who can hear the will of God and do it*.[36]

The same author deals with the woman-as-wife stereotype when discussing Mark 12:18-25 and its parallel texts in Matthew and Luke. That is the familiar story of the Sadducces who posed to Jesus the question of the man who died and left a wife, but no children. She was then married in succession by six brothers of her late husband, all of whom died leaving no issue. The question that the Sadducees posed was, whose wife will she be in the resurrection? And Jesus' answer is well known: "When they rise from the dead, they neither marry nor are given in marriage, but are like angels in heaven."

This text is usually interpreted in the sense that in heaven there will be no sexuality. Some males have even understood it to mean that in heaven women will be unnecessary! But when a woman reads this text, she sees much more in it. The question posed by the Sadducees was based on the view of a woman as primarily a wife and someone's possession. It is significant that the question does not start by referring to "a woman who was widowed," but to "seven brothers." The important question is not what will happen to the woman herself. The question is rather that she *belongs* to seven different brothers in this life, and that therefore in the next it will be difficult to decide the issue of to which of the seven brothers she belongs. For all intents and purposes, the story could have been about seven brothers who successively inherited a cow from each other. A woman who knows that society stereotypes a woman as "someone's wife" will see in this text much more than will a man.

A woman hears about a durable woman who outlived seven husbands. A woman hears that this person was someone's property—*seven someones*.

A woman hears that this someone was passed from brother to brother perhaps without her approval, because it was the Deuteronomic law and custom.

A woman understands that not having children would have placed an added stigma on the woman.

A woman hears that Jesus, although he says nothing about levirate marriage, disclaims the dependency of the marriage bond in the resurrection.

A woman hears Jesus declaring that she is not someone's property, that she has equal status in the resurrection, that she has a position not relative to anyone else. She is a spiritual being. At least in heaven she will not achieve her identity through someone else.[37]

From the Third World come other insights. Some of these are startlingly profound in their simplicity. Take for instance the words of Catholic Bishop Christopher Mwoleka of Tanzania:

I think we have problems understanding the Holy Trinity because we approach the mystery from the wrong side. The intellectual side is not the best side to start with. We try to get hold of the wrong end of the stick, and it never works. The right approach to the mystery is to *imitate* the Trinity. We keep making the mistake Philip made by asking: "Rabbi, show us the Father!" Christ was dismayed by the question and rebuked Philip: "Philip, have I been with you so long and yet you don't know me? He who has seen me has seen the Father. How can you say: show us the Father? Do you not believe that I am in the Father and the Father in me?" The Christ continued to say: "He who believes in me will also do the works that I do, and greater works than these will he do."

On believing in this mystery, the first thing we should have done was to imitate God, then we would ask no more questions, for we would understand. God does not reveal Himself to us for the sake of speculation. He is not giving us a riddle to solve. He is offering us life. He is telling us: "This is what it means to live, now begin to live as I do." What is the one and only reason why God revealed this mystery to us if it is not to stress that life is not life at all unless it is shared?

If we would once begin to share life in all its aspects, we would soon understand what the Trinity is all about and rejoice. . . .

Why did God upon creating human beings not put us straight into heaven, but instead put us here on earth? The reason why we should first have to wait here for a number of years before going to heaven would seem to be that we should practice and acquire some competence in the art of sharing life. Without this practice we are apt to mess up things in heaven. . . . All I want to say is this: it is by sharing the earthly goods that we come to have an idea of what it will be like to share the life of God.

As long as we do not know how to share earthly goods, as God would have us do, it is an illusion to imagine that we know what it is to share the life of the Trinity which is our destiny. . . .

The question is: Have we imitated the Holy Trinity in sharing earthly goods? . . . Could I truthfully say: "All mine are thine, and thine are mine," to each and all? This is what we are supposed to imitate (John 17:10). Then in what sense can we be said to be practicing to live the life of God? How can we dare to profess the religion of the Trinity?[38]

As we read these words, do we not sense a kinship between the Tanzanian bishop and some of the writers that we quoted in the previous section, such as Ambrose and Basil the Great? Is it a mere coincidence that those theologians of old, who so stressed the need for a different social order, were also among the champions of Trinitarian theology? Or could it be that we have been misled in our reading of the history of theology, and that the doctrine of the Trinity, far from being the purely speculative matter that we have been led to believe, was part and parcel of those preachers' radical theology? This is an intriguing question which would bear investigation. But in any case, there is no doubt that Bishop Mwoleka has given us an insight into the significance of Trinitarian theology that we are not likely to derive from many of the supposedly more sophisticated Western theologians.

For too long the theological and ecclesiastical establishment of the North Atlantic has been doing theology as if the rest of the world did not exist or had only the secondary sort of existence of the Lone Ranger's Tonto. What is currently happening is that Tonto has finally decided to speak up and is making much more sense than the Lone Ranger ever did. The Lone Ranger, with his mask, his white horse, and his flashy gear, thought that he knew all about doing justice. But Tonto is telling him that one can only know injustice when one suffers it. The only way one can have real access to the resources mentioned in this chapter, and to others like them, is to join the Tontos of our day in the struggle against injustice, and to join them in such a way as to be deprived of white horses and flashy gear. Do-gooder preaching is out. Cries of "hi ho, Silver" will no longer do. The word of the gospel today, as in the times of Jesus, as ever, comes to us most clearly in the painful groans of the oppressed. We must listen to those groans. We must join the struggle to the point where we too must groan. Or we may choose the other alternative, which is not to hear the gospel at all.

IV. SOME POINTERS
ON BIBLICAL INTERPRETATION

In the foregoing chapters, while discussing various issues, we have given a number of examples of the manner in which liberation theologies interpret various passages of the Bible. We have also shown that, both in earlier Christian tradition and in contemporary sources, a preacher of liberation can find insights regarding the meaning of the Bible and its message. But we have also insisted that liberation preachers, particularly white males who do not form part as yet of a liberation movement, must not rely on those resources to do their biblical interpretation for them. If they have truly been involved in the hermeneutic circle, and developed the ideological and exegetical suspicion that comes out of such involvement, they will soon find themselves discovering dimensions in the Bible that they did not realize were there. But in spite of this, as exercises or pointers to help develop a liberation hermeneutic, there are a number of suggestions that can be made.

ASK THE POLITICAL QUESTION

If it is true that liberation theology is that which develops out of the experience of the powerless as they are being empowered by God, the political question is the first one that we must ask as we approach any biblical passage. Obviously, "political" is not understood here in the common sense of whether to vote for one candidate or another, although it does have to do with that. By "political" we mean rather the interplay of power, the question of who is expected to have authority over whom, or of who is an "insider" and who is not. But "political" means above all, in this context, the manner in which God intervenes in such relations, and how God responds to the power or powerlessness of various individuals or groups of people. To ask this question at the outset may serve to counteract the opposite, more common interpretation, which acts as if such matters were of no consequence, and thus serves to entrench the powerful in their positions of privilege.

In some cases the political dimension is rather evident. Such is, for instance, the case of the prophet Amos in his relationship to Jeroboam, king of Israel, and to Amaziah, the priest of Bethel, which culminates in Amos 7:12-15:

> And Amaziah said to Amos, "O seer, go, flee away to the land of Judah, and eat bread there, and prophesy there; but never again prophesy at Bethel, for it is the king's sanctuary, and it is a temple of the kingdom."
> Then Amos answered Amaziah, "I am no prophet, nor a prophet's son; but I am a herdsman, and a dresser of sycamore trees, and the Lord took me from following the flock, and the Lord said to me, 'Go, prophesy to my people Israel.' " (RSV)

At least one aspect of the political situation in this text is often pointed out when preachers note that the priest at Bethel was afraid of the implications of what Amos was saying, and that Amaziah was the mouthpiece of official religion, which as usual was being used to uphold the status quo. But what is often missed is that Amaziah attempted to use the power and prestige of Jeroboam to silence the disturbing prophet. Thus, it is not simply a matter of official religion supporting the structures of oppression, but also of those structures supporting that religion which it finds most useful. There is, however, another dimension that is hardly ever noticed. When Amos says that he is not a prophet nor a prophet's son, but a herdsman and a dresser of sycamore trees, he is not saying simply that God called him to preach out of another occupation. Altogether too often is this text used to highlight the experience of a middle-aged and successful businessman who leaves his company in order to become a minister. And it may well be that such a man has a genuine call, but to apply this text to that situation is to miss the point of what Amos is saying. He is not simply telling Amaziah that he was doing something else when God called him. He is rather responding to the priest's ominous words from the perspective of a powerless one whom God has called and empowered. Amaziah tells him that he is interfering with what is going on at Bethel, "the king's sanctuary, and it is a temple of the kingdom." He also suggests that the prophet return to his native Judah, which was not as affluent nor as cultured as Israel, and that he prophesy there—which, after all, is his home turf. Amaziah's words are thus both a threat and a putdown. The prophet's response shows how he must speak and reject the priest's suggestion, not because he himself has power or authority, but because he has been empowered from on high. He says, in effect, "You are a priest, and I do not even belong to the class of the professional prophets. I am nothing but a herdsman and an agricultural laborer. And out of that situation, in backward Judah, the Lord took me and sent me to prophesy to mighty, rich, and proud Israel." When all these political dimensions are seen, the text has a bite that it did not have when we simply applied it to the successful businessman turned preacher.

In other cases the political dimension may not be as evident; but it is still there. Take for instance the story of Rahab, as told in the book of Joshua. The fact that she was a harlot is the one detail that all remember, either because it rubs against their moral standards or because it appeals to their prurient interests. Others point out that through her faith her entire family was saved, and establish a parallel with the jailer at Philippi. But few take note of the political dimensions involved in this story. What we have here is simply a case of treason. Rahab betrays the people of Jericho, her city. It may well be at this point that her being a harlot is significant. The word used for her is not the one which refers to the more respected religious prostitutes. As a harlot, although perhaps not as condemned as modern prostitutes, she certainly was not one of the powerful in Jericho. And when the opportunity came, she sided with the God who empowered the nomadic and, from the point of view of Jericho, semibarbaric Israelites. It is significant that John Calvin, who had to leave his beloved country because of his faith, saw the political dimensions in Rahab's action and saw also that faith may lead one to break the civil law:

> When, therefore, Rahab knew that the object intended was the overthrow of the city in which she had been born and brought up, it seems a detestable act of inhumanity to give her aid and counsel to the spies. . . . Therefore, although she had been bound to her countrymen up to that very day, yet when she was adopted into the body of the Church, her new condition was a kind of manumission from the common law by which citizens are bound toward each other.[1]

We have already referred to the story of Simon Magus in Acts 8. It is noteworthy that, although the text itself says that Simon "amazed the nation of Samaria," and that all, "from the least to the greatest," said of him that "this man is that power of God which is called Great," the standard interpretation of the entire incident leaves aside all question of power and powerlessness and prefers to speak of Simon as a hypocrite, when the text says nothing about that. In fact, what the text does say is that Simon believed and was baptized, and that he who used to amaze all was himself amazed. When we therefore ask the political question of this text, it would seem that Simon Magus' problems had to do with power, rather than with disbelief or hypocrisy. And then the intervention of Simon Peter, the ignorant fisherman from Galilee, takes on a new shade of meaning.

Still in Acts 8, the reader may wish to ask the political question of the other major incident in that chapter, the encounter between Philip and the Ethiopian eunuch. Was the latter an insider, an outsider, or both? What does the text say about his standing in Ethiopia? What do we infer about his standing in Judaism, on the basis of what the Law said about eunuchs? He was reading the prophet Isaiah. What does that prophet have to say about eunuchs and foreigners? In the light of all this, what is the significance of Philip's willingness to baptize this man? What does this say about the nature and mission of the church vis-à-vis the various rules of exclusion in our society?

It would be possible to multiply *ad infinitum* the examples of texts that become clearer when one poses the political question. But the point of this section is more than that. The entire Bible must be read in the light of that question. And this is borne out by the fact that the crucial saving events in both the Old and New Testaments cannot be understood aside from it.

In the Old Testament, the escape from Egypt is an eminently political event. More than that, it is an event in which, to use the words of Mary much later, God "has shown strength with his arm, he has scattered the proud in the imagination of their hearts, he has put down the mighty from their thrones, and exalted those of low degree" (Luke 1:51-52, RSV). Apart from that political dimension, the first chapters of the book of Exodus make no sense. And it is a political dimension in which, as Mary saw clearly, God works in a definite direction, against the might of Pharaoh and for the oppressed children of Israel.

Some will respond to this that such is clearly the case in the Old Testament, which is "materialistic" and lacks the "spiritual" insight of the New. But, aside from the fact that the church very early rejected such contraposition of the two Testaments as heretical, the New Testament is just as political. It is in part to show this that we have quoted the song of Mary—of Mary, who is usually depicted in quiet, submissive tones that seem to fade into the background! But the entire story of Jesus is profoundly political. God's choice to be born in a stable, to a carpenter's family, rather than in the home of a king or priest, manifests God's politics. We have already referred to the political naiveté of the magi and its tragic consequences. Luke also states that Jesus was born in Bethlehem because Augustus had decreed a census. And Matthew tells us that Jesus was an exile, not only in Egypt, but also throughout his early life, since the reason why he grew up in Nazareth was that he could not return to Judea, then under the authority of Herod's son, Archelaus (Matt. 2:22-23). When Jesus set out on his public ministry, he was constantly at odds with the religious establishment, with which he had a long series of highly political encounters.

One such encounter deserves a separate paragraph, since it has so often been used by those whose political interests lead them to claim that Jesus wanted his followers to accept the existing order of things. It is the incident which concluded with Jesus' words: "Render to

Caesar the things that are Caesar's, and to God the things that are God's" (Mark 12:13-17 and parallels). What the supposedly "apolitical" interpreters fail to see is the radically subversive note in Jesus' answer. He did not simply say that it was lawful to pay taxes, and that then one could go on to religious things. What he said was that the entire monetary system, because it bore the likeness and the inscription of Caesar, was to be sent back to Caesar, rejected, set aside. He actually refused to condone the practice of those who thought they could cherish Caesar's money, be involved without asking any questions of the entire system, and then debate as to whether they ought to pay taxes or not![2]

In the end, these various encounters led to the very political events of the arrest, the trial, and the crucifixion. Caiaphas, Herod, and Pilate are not mere props in a story which would unfold without them. They are main actors. Without them the Gospel narrative would make no sense. And then, beyond the arrest, beyond the trial, beyond the crucifixion, come the most political events in the entire Bible, which God "accomplished in Christ when he raised him from the dead and made him sit at his right hand in the heavenly places, far above all rule and authority and power and dominion, and above every name that is named, not only in this age but also in that which is to come" (Eph. 1:20-21, RSV). To call an outlawed and crucified carpenter King of kings and Lord of lords (Rev. 19:16) is a highly political statement.

REASSIGN THE CAST OF CHARACTERS

Whenever we hear or read a narrative and seek to derive from it some meaning for ourselves, the message conveyed by the story depends in part on where we place ourselves in it. This can be seen clearly in the case of the encounter between King David and the prophet Nathan, after David had Uriah killed so he could take Bathsheba (II Sam. 12:1-15). As is well known, Nathan tells David the story of a rich man who had many sheep, but who killed his poor neighbor's pet lamb in order to feed a visitor. David is enraged and says to Nathan: "As the Lord lives, the man who has done this deserves to die" (12:5). And it is at this point that Nathan brings the parable home to the king: "You are the man. Thus says the Lord, the God of Israel, 'I anointed you king over Israel, . . .' " (12:7). What has taken place here is that David has been forced to change the place where he put himself in the story. As long as he thought that the prophet had come to him to ask him for justice on behalf of another, he saw himself as the king who was to judge the rich man. But suddenly Nathan tells him that he is the rich man, that it is he that has abused his power, that it is he that, by his own verdict, deserves to die. Thus, the manner in which David assigns the cast of characters in the story has everything to do with the meaning of the story for him. In one case he is the king, the judge, who responds in righteous anger. In the other he is the oppressor who has used his power unjustly and who therefore can only respond, "I have sinned against the Lord" (12:13).

The same change of meaning takes place for us when we reassign the cast of characters in the parables of Jesus. Many of them are directed against the blindness of the religious leaders of the time, who could not see the inbreaking of the Kingdom in the teachings and actions of Jesus. When we read those parables, our normal reaction is to take for granted that, since we are followers of Jesus, we understand what they are all about. Today's Pharisees are those who reject Jesus, who do not attend church, who make a living by peddling pornography, etc. But is this really so? In Jesus' time there were also many who were irreligious or pagan; but the parables were not critical of them. In Jesus' time there were also those who did not keep the religious observances set forth in the Law and who hardly ever went to the Temple; but the parables do not attack them. In Jesus' time there were prostitutes; but the parables do not heap on them the contempt that society felt for them. Surprisingly, Jesus' parables are not directed against the sins of the irreligious, but rather against the sins of the religious, and particularly against their refusal to see the inbreaking of the Kingdom. When we realize this and reassign the cast of characters, particularly if we do it on the basis of the question of power and powerlessness, the parables may take on a very different meaning, which may be closer to the original.

This is true of the entire Bible, both as a whole and in its various parts. Since liberation theologians see the Bible as above all a book of history—the history of God's liberating acts—the point at which we identify with that history is of crucial importance.

Let us look again at the story of Simon Magus in Acts 8, to which we referred in the previous section, and see how the text looks as we assign the cast of characters in different ways. Our normal reaction is to think that Simon Magus is whoever is opposing the church, or whoever is teaching incorrect doctrine. As a matter of fact, since a very early date in the history of the church Simon Magus has become an ecclesiastical scapegoat. He was the father of all heresies. In the Middle Ages, the practice of buying and selling ecclesiastical offices was dubbed "simony," after Simon Magus. What this means is that we identify immediately with the hero of the story, Simon Peter, and place our enemies in the role of Simon Magus.

But there are other characters with whom we could identify or that we should at least try on for size. One of these is Philip, who apparently received Simon Magus into the church without asking too many questions. Do we not allow ourselves to be overwhelmed by the power and prestige of the powerful, to the point that we are hesitant to ask of them the proper questions? Has not the church throughout its history received many a potentate and given them authority within the Christian community, without forcing them to face up to the radical demands of the gospel? When we assign ourselves to the role of Philip, the entire story takes on a different meaning. But, then, should we not look also at the possibility that we may be in a position similar to that of Simon Magus? If at this point we ask the question of power and powerlessness, it may well be that, at least in the context of the distribution of wealth throughout the world, we are in the position of Simon Magus. Our North American society and the church which is a part of it have grown accustomed to having all be amazed at our power. When we read the text in this light, it tells us that we must beware of the Philips who are willing to preach the message to us, without showing us that to accept that message means to accept an entirely different ordering of power, and that we must be willing to hear the word of God as it comes to us through the Simon Peters of today's world—the fisherfolk on a lake in Nicaragua, the political prisoners in South Africa, the women whose rights are trampled.

At this point the reader may wish to choose a narrative passage in Scripture and see what are the various ways in which a cast of characters can be assigned. Take, for instance, II Kings 6:8-28. Again, we may be tempted to identify ourselves with the prophet Elisha, who knows the plans of the enemy before they execute them, and who can see the invisible hosts of the Lord. But try placing yourself (and your congregation) in the place of the servant who sees only the armies of the enemy and for whose enlightenment Elisha prays. In what sense is this a better point of identification? Can you and your congregation somehow play the role of the host of horses and chariots of fire that surrounded the enemy? Or perhaps even of the king of Syria and his armies? What political realities, both in the text and in today's situation, would seem to make one or another of these points of identification more adequate? And, once we have identified our own role, who among our contemporaries plays the other roles?

This perspective-taking, however, must not be used as an excuse for allegorizing, about which we shall have more to say later on. Allegorizing avoids the concrete, political setting of the text and of its hearers. This is the opposite. Take into account the setting in both the text and the contemporary situation before you decide on an assignment of roles.

Most often that decision is made quite unconsciously and reflects where we stand in society. In a summer school at Perkins School of Theology some time ago, we asked a group of students to name some of the passages that had meant the most for them. Interestingly enough, a large number of them chose Luke 4:18-19, where Jesus reads and applies to himself the words of Isaiah: "The Spirit of the Lord is upon me, . . ." What was most interesting, however, was that white males who chose this passage invariably interpreted it as referring to their call to ministry. The Spirit of the Lord had anointed them to preach good news to the poor, etc. But those among the women and the minority men who chose the same text interpreted it quite differently. What was important to them was that Jesus had been anointed to bring good news to them, to proclaim release to them, etc. In short, those who were used to being in positions of privilege identified at one place, while those whose experience was the opposite identified at another. Had the white males tried the exercise of changing the cast of characters, they might have come to realize how close their interpretation was to a Messiah complex!

A liberation preacher soon comes to ask the question of the cast of characters almost automatically, and then comes to the realization that this sort of question must be asked, not only of particular texts, but also of the entire thrust of biblical history. Why is it that in Christian communities even the most powerful think that they stand with the children of Israel and do not see that in many ways they are closer to Pharaoh than to Moses and his host? Why is it that so many preachers, when approaching a prophetic text, take for granted that they are the prophets, and the congregation is the disobedient Israel that must be chastized? Why is it that so many secure, prosperous congregations can read the psalms that deal with powerlessness or with political persecution as if they were the powerless and the persecuted? Why is it that so many religious folk can listen to the teachings of Jesus as if they were the despised publicans and harlots that will go first into the Kingdom? If the question of power and powerlessness is fundamental in order to understand the message of Scripture, the manner in which that question may be brought home to us is through the way in which we assign the characters in the biblical account.

IMAGINE A DIFFERENT SETTING

Another manner in which a preacher of liberation can gain new insight into the meaning of a text is to imagine it being studied and expounded in a different socio-political setting. In the last chapter we gave some examples of how the Bible is read differently when seen from the perspective of people whose political setting is different. Reading such books as *The Gospel in Solentiname* and *Jesus According to a Woman* will give the liberation preacher a number of examples of biblical texts seen from a different perspective. But, since this is something which the preacher must do Sunday after Sunday, it will be very difficult to find actual interpretations from other perspectives for every text. It is at this point that the liberation preacher might imagine the same text being read in different circumstances.

Some examples should clarify what this means. Take for instance the 23rd Psalm. We all know that psalm by heart, and we know exactly in what sort of setting to use it. Because it speaks of the "valley of the shadow of death," and because of its generally comforting character, we read it at funerals. Because of the shepherding and bucolic imagery of the first verses, we read it whenever we feel harassed and anxious. And there is no doubt that there is much in the psalm that commends this usage. But the liberation preacher who intends to preach on this psalm will profit by imagining it set in different circumstances. Imagine, for instance, this psalm being read in an underground church in Nazi Germany, in the context of a communion service. In that scenario what stands out is not only the valley of the shadow of death, but also the table prepared in the presence of the enemies—an image that is hardly appropriate at a funeral, and that is therefore usually glossed over. But then change the setting and imagine this psalm being read by a group of Christians in a slum in the Dominican Republic, who are hungry because a North American company has taken over their land in order to plant sugar cane, and who have been forced to move to the slums in the capital. At that point, the table in the psalm becomes an expression that God will indeed fill a very real need. It becomes impossible to read the psalm as if there were no reference to food in it. And immediately the next step is taken: the "enemies" become very real. It is interesting that many Western, affluent Christians are embarrassed by the reference to the enemies in that psalm. Many a sermon in such affluent settings either glosses over the "enemies" or interprets them allegorically as temptations. But our hungry Dominican sisters and brothers will not see the text in that fashion. They are really hungry. They are hungry because they have enemies—perhaps not enemies who hate them, but nevertheless enemies who are destroying them. To them, a very significant part of the promise of the psalm is that they shall be fed, and that such feeding will also be a vindication before their enemies. And, given the situation of today's world, we may be the enemy to whom they are referring! Thus, imagining the psalm being read and interpreted in a different setting will lead the liberation preacher to assign the cast of characters in a very different way than would be the case without such an exercise.

What the liberation preacher seeks to do by applying this

methodology is to restore the text to its original setting, or at least to one that is politically similar to it. Very often a text is made more oppressive by reading it in a setting that is very different from the original one. This is the case with the three passages of the New Testament dealing with household legislation to which we have already referred (Eph. 5:21–6:9; Col. 3:18–4:1; I Peter 2:18–3:7). One of the ways in which these passages have been made very oppressive is by taking them out of the original context in which they were intended to be read. Thus, there are today many groups of women who gather to study God's will for them, and who take as their point of departure what these texts say about the submissive role of wives. But in reading these texts in such separate groups, these women are missing what was also part of the original text and its situation, that is, that at the same time that the wives were listening to these words they were also overhearing the words addressed to their husbands, which clearly limited the use of their power.

In a similar manner, these texts were used a few generations ago in order to instill in slaves a spirit of acceptance of their condition. But in such cases what very often took place was that the slaves were read only the words addressed to them, and not those directed at the masters, who are told, for instance, to "do the same to them" (Eph. 6:9). In some places there are still churches standing where the slave gallery had a high wall in front of it, allowing the slaves to see only the altar and the pulpit, but not their masters. The reason for this was that a slave-owning society was keenly aware of the need to avoid having the slaves see their masters kneeling! But in the early church the slaves did see the masters—or at least any such as were present—kneeling. And therefore the words of the New Testament, intended to be read and applied in such socially mixed company, came to have a different meaning when read in a setting which was intentionally segregated between masters and slaves—or, in our day between males and females in the case of some groups who advocate the submission of wives.

At another point we shall have opportunity to return to these texts and to show further what a liberation interpretation of them would be. But here the main point is simply that we must make certain that the socio-political setting in which a particular text is being interpreted does not turn it into an excuse for oppression, rather than a word of liberation.

Since the Lone-Ranger Bible study is out, the liberation preacher can enlist the help of others in the congregation, or outside of it, in this process of imagining a different setting. For instance, the male preacher can gain insight from the manner in which the women of his congregation, particularly those who are aware of the need for a new interpretation of the Bible, understand a particular text. Very few male interpreters would have been aware of the manner in which Jesus rejected the stereotype of woman as mother and wife in the two texts discussed in the last chapter. But this theme would soon have surfaced in a group of women applying their experience and their feelings to the study of the Bible.

To find a different setting in matters of race and class, unfortunately most preachers will have to go beyond the resources of the congregation. But here again the white preacher can ask ethnic minority colleagues or lay persons how they react to a particular text, and particularly how they react to the interpretation which the preacher intends to give it. Figuratively speaking, this is a way of placing the text in a different socio-political setting and seeing what comes out in that different context.

This definitely does not mean that the liberation preacher will then proceed to preach on the meaning of the text in that other setting. To do so would be to deny the basic principle that liberation theology must always be concrete. To preach in Atlanta, Georgia, to a white middle-class congregation, a sermon about the meaning of the 23rd Psalm for the hungry in the slums of the Dominican Republic may be very enlightening about the conditions of hunger in that country, and how they deny the worth of the human creature; but it will not be liberation preaching. What the liberation preacher will do in this case is to take note of the insights gained by placing the text in the context of hunger in the Dominican Republic and then return to the concrete situation of a particular congregation in Atlanta, in order to see what the text has to say here. Why does the Atlanta congregation—and the Atlanta preacher, apart from this exercise—fail to see in the text what is so evident in the Dominican Republic? Investigating that failure, the white liberation preacher in

Atlanta may see a sign of the nature of the oppression under which
the North American congregation lives. Its oppression will
undoubtedly be of a different degree and quality than that of the
Dominican peasant. But still, it is that oppression, and the manner
in which it conspires with the much greater oppression of the
Dominican peasant, that must be addressed in Atlanta. Otherwise
we are still at the rather innocuous level of the do-gooder liberal
preacher.

CONSIDER THE DIRECTION OF THE ACTION

There are many portions of the Bible which have repeatedly
caused difficulties for interpreters. Even before the advent of
Christianity, there were difficulties in Judaism regarding various
laws that seemed terribly crass to the cultured Hellenistic mind. The
solution found by many Jews, particularly in Alexandria, was to
interpret Scripture allegorically. Later, when Christians had to face
the same sort of difficulty, there were those, again mostly in
Alexandria, who had recourse to the same method.

Such allegorical interpretation, however, is less than useless. By
determining what different elements in the biblical narrative or in the
laws mean, the interpreter ends up determining what is to be found in
Scripture—very much like the magician who surreptitiously places a
rabbit inside a hat, and then pulls it out in public with much fanfare.
The net result of such procedure is that the Bible comes to naught, and
what is actually preached and taught is the opinion of the person who
determines what the symbols mean. Therefore, it is not surprising that
the Jewish and Christian Alexandrians who interpreted the Bible
allegorically claimed that it essentially coincided with the Platonism of
the time, to which they were devoted. Nor is it surprising that
allegorical interpretation has been, and still is today, one of the main
ways in which the commonly accepted values and ordering of society
manage to pose as biblically inspired.

But having said that, we must still deal with the many passages of
Scripture whose relevance for today it is difficult to see. There are the
laws about slavery, the injunction that women must cover their
heads when they preach, with its counterpart that a man's head

remain uncovered (I Cor. 11:5), the seemingly contradictory order that women are to keep silent in church, the instruction that younger widows are to remarry, have children, and keep house, and many others.

The usual way in which liberal interpreters dispose of such difficulties is to declare that they simply reflect the culture of the time when the Bible was written. But such a solution will not do. It will not do, first of all, because it is a truism which can be universally applied. There is no doubt that the culture of the times can be seen in these passages. But there is also no doubt that it can be seen in every single portion of the Bible, from the first chapter of Genesis to the last of Revelation, including such beloved texts as the parables of Jesus and John 3:16! Secondly, this explanation will not do because it places twentieth century culture in the privileged position of being able to decide what in the biblical past was culturally determined, and what was not. The Bible never says: "This is culturally determined and therefore can be ignored." Nor does it say about other passages: "This is absolute, eternal, immutable truth, which is valid in every cultural setting." Finally, such a solution, precisely because it makes our culture the ultimate judge as to what portions of the Bible are still valid, and which are not, eventually means that the Bible no longer has a word from outside, and we are simply left with the usual type of theology, which does little more than reflect the present situation and therefore ultimately works in favor of the oppressors.

The manner in which liberation theology approaches this situation—and indeed the entire Bible—is by insisting on the historical character of revelation. Truth in the Bible is understood in a very different manner than it is sought by the philosophers who look for immutable essences. Truth in the Bible is God active in history. In consequence, what we must seek in Scripture is not immutable essences, nor eternal laws, but rather the record of God's action in history. And this action does not take place in some special domain of "salvation history"—what the Germans call *Heilsgeschichte*—but in the very history of which we and all humankind are a part.

Ignacio Ellacuría has ably stated what this means for our understanding of revelation:

Now the communication of a living God in history means that this
communication must be concerned with the history of human beings and
that it must be so in a changing and progressive way. The two statements
are interrelated. Without God's irruption into history, without his
presence in the historical realm, we would know very little about him. But
if his presence is to be found in the historical realm, then we must be open
to this changing irruption which is history.[3]

What this means is that, when reading a text in Scripture, we are
not to see it as a gem floating in a void, but rather place it in its
historical setting and ask the question of the direction of God's action
in that text. Then, and only then, can we seek to apply the text to our
own time.

Since several of the examples quoted above have to do with either
slavery or the place of women in the church and in society, it may be
well to show what this principle means by applying it to a passage
which deals with slaves and with women, and to which we have had
occasion to refer already.

Ephesians 5:21–6:9 is the most detailed of the three main texts in
the New Testament dealing with "household legislation." This text
is usually interpreted in one of two ways. Some take it to be absolute,
immutable law and on that basis claim that the submission of wives
to husbands is part of the changeless will of God. Others say that
what we have here is an expression of the culture of the times, and
therefore ought to be disregarded. The first position is hardly tenable
when, as we have suggested earlier, the instructions regarding slaves
and masters are seen as an integral part of the passage. To say that this
text proves that the submission of wives to their husbands is part of
the immutable will of God would immediately imply that the same is
true of slavery. The second position is tempting, for it would allow us
to do away with the uncomfortable passage about slaves. But then
one would still be left with the question of whether or not wives
ought to submit to their husbands. And the answer to that question
would depend, not on the text itself, but on the interpreter's decision
as to whether that particular injunction is an expression of the
culture of the times or of the immutable will of God. Along these
lines of debate, the biblical text itself soon loses all relevance.

Liberation theology would lead to interpreting this text—as well as any other—along historical lines. In other words, the liberation interpreter does not look for an immutable law to be applied in any situation, nor does such an interpreter simply discount uncomfortable passages by claiming that they are no longer relevant. Rather, one must begin by looking at the concrete situation in which these words were written, see in what direction they point given that situation, and then follow the same direction in today's world.

In the case of the text in question, what we must first ask is what was the situation of wives, children, and slaves at the time of this writing. Obviously, this presents some difficulties in this particular case, for scholars are not agreed as to the date of authorship of this document, nor as to who were its intended readers—the words "in Ephesus" in 1:1 do not appear in a number of important manuscripts. But in any case it seems likely that this document was written sometime in the second half of the first century, and that its context is the Eastern portion of the Empire—probably around Asia Minor.

The institution of marriage had been changing in the last years of the Roman Republic and the beginning of the Empire.[4] But these changes had taken place mostly in the West. In the East, the ancient Greek customs regarding marriage still held sway, often supported by a stricter interpretation of Roman law than was current even in Rome. In the Greek tradition, marriage was a very unequal relationship. For instance, men were allowed to have concubines, but if a woman committed adultery her husband was expected at least to divorce her, and both custom and law allowed him to kill her. Also women were confined to their own homes, and even there they were expected to remain in the section reserved for them, where very few males ever entered. Although in the western portion of the Roman Empire things had begun to change, the old Roman law also had a very unequal understanding of marriage, and in the East the conservatism of the region found support in such laws. According to the ancient power of *manus*, the chief of a family had absolute authority over his own wife—and those of his sons. He could punish her disobedience even by death or by selling her into slavery. And her status was so low that she had no legal standing, to the point that her husband was legally responsible for her actions. In one kind of marriage, the contract took the form of a sale with the groom's father—or the groom himself, if he was a free agent—sealing the contract with a down payment. On such occasions, the groom gave his bride a ring, as a symbol of the purchase price. By the first century, there were some limitations put on the power of a husband over his wife. For instance, in order to encourage population growth, Augustus decreed that any matron with three or more children would be granted a number of legal rights. But such a law, which saw women as reproductive machines, can hardly be said to have been a great advance toward a more balanced situation in marriage. In any case, in spite of the changing laws, the basic institution of marriage still saw the wife as a property and ward of her husband, and any laws protecting her were mere reflections of the laws protecting children—for instance, a great advancement was made when wives were allowed to inherit their husbands' estates on the same basis as did minor children!

The relationship between fathers and their children was similar to that between husbands and wives. When we read the text in Ephesians, and others like it, we take for granted that "children" here refers to minors. But such would not necessarily be the case at that time. According to Roman law, the oldest male member of the family, the *pater familias*, had the right of *manus* over all his children for life. A father had the right to determine whether a newly born child would be allowed to live or not. In the early years of the Christian church, it was still customary for poor children to be exposed—that is, left out to die—by their fathers, who did not have the means to support them. And rich fathers often decided to expose their sons in order not to divide the inheritance. Even after it was decided that the child would live, the *pater familias* had the right to kill or sell it. That right was seldom exercised, and there were attempts to limit it by law. But as late as the fourth century it still existed.

Likewise, a son could hold no property as long as his father lived—a daughter's case was somewhat different, for on her marriage she came under the jurisdiction of her husband's *pater familias*. And any money the son made, even if it was as a high government official or a general, belonged to his father. The same was true of all legal rights, which were vested in the father for as long as they both lived.

Besides the death of the *pater familias*, there was one other way in which a son could be freed from such a dependent situation. That was a legal process called "emancipation." To do this, a father had to sell his son to a friend, who then returned him. After doing this three times, the father could declare the son "emancipated." But even then the son was not entirely free, for he now stood in a relationship to his father similar to that between a freed slave and a former master.

The condition of slaves was obviously worse. A slave had no rights and could be shamed, tortured, or killed at the master's whim. A slave's word had no standing in court, unless the deposition had been obtained through the use of torture. An untractable slave was often put to death, usually by crucifixion. If any dared raise their hand against their master, not only the guilty party, but any other slaves who happened to be under the same roof at the time were condemned to death. Often elderly slaves were expelled from the household to die of hunger.

Like a child, a slave could be freed. Some slaves were able to save enough money to buy their own freedom. Others were manumitted —set free—by their masters. In ancient Rome, a slave could be manumitted simply by being invited to sit at the master's table. But Imperial Rome wished to preserve the institution of slavery and took steps to make manumission much more difficult. The number of slaves that could be set free at one time was curtailed. And Augustus decreed that no slave under thirty could be set free, except in the case of extraordinary service—such as saving the master's life—which had to be proven before the law. (This may be a point to take into consideration when studying the Epistle to Philemon, for if Onesimus was under thirty there was no way in which his master could legally set him free.) Older slaves could buy their freedom by paying their masters with their own savings. But this was possible only if the master permitted it, for legally those savings also belonged to the *pater familias*.

Even freed slaves did not have the status of free citizens. They still remained in a special relationship of dependency to their former masters. If a freed slave died without leaving children, the inheritance went to the former master—the *patronus*. And in any case the freed slave had a number of obligations toward the *patronus*, which had to be fulfilled under penalty of being sold back into slavery.

Such were the conditions that obtained at the time of the writing of the Epistle to the Ephesians. One half of each of the three pairs mentioned—wives, children, slaves—had practically no rights, while the other half—husbands, fathers, masters—had all the rights and the power. When we then read the passage in question with this background in mind, we find that what stands out is not the words to the powerless, because their relationship to the powerful was taken for granted. Indeed, to have said anything else would have made the document and its author, as well as any church which read it in its gatherings, liable to prosecution for sedition and disregard for the law. So, the author stays within the bounds of the law in telling wives, children, and slaves to fulfill their obligations.

But then come the words to the powerful. What in essence such words say is that the powerful ought not to abuse their power, and that the reason for this is that there is Another more powerful than they, who demands just treatment for the powerless. Thus, the husbands are clearly reminded that they are part of the bride of Christ, that is, that they too have a husband. And the masters are reminded that they too have a master. On this basis, husbands and wives, fathers and children, masters and slaves are to "be subject to one another out of reverence for Christ" (5:21), and masters are to act toward slaves in the same way that slaves are required to act toward them (6:8).

And these words are intended to be read, not to slaves, children, and wives first, and then to masters, fathers, and husbands, but to all together. Short of actual sedition, it is hard to imagine what more revolutionary words could be written at that time!

All of this clarifies for us the *direction* of the text. And it is that direction that it all important. At that particular time in history, these words were subverting the established order of inequality and injustice. To use them to uphold today whatever remains of such injustice in family relations would be to use them in a direction absolutely contrary to their intention. What we must do is exactly the opposite. These words invite us to examine our contemporary relationships, see what in them is unjust, and be certain that God's will opposes such injustice.

In conclusion, in interpreting any text a preacher of liberation avoids taking it as concrete and immutable instructions for every situation, but rather inquires after the direction of the action in its original setting and then seeks to act, and to invite others to act, in the same direction.

AVOID AVOIDANCE

The most common way in which traditional preaching and theology avoid dealing with the issues of liberation is by evading those texts where such issues are most obvious. Most of the current lectionaries, since they have been prepared from the same perspective, abet this. Therefore, liberation preachers may want to examine the texts assigned in the lectionary for a certain length of time—perhaps an entire year—and preach on some of the texts that seem to have been avoided.

Lectionaries, however, have a decided value in that, by including readings from both the Old and the New Testament, they force the attention of the church upon both of them. Even after having condemned Marcionism, which rejected the Old Testament, Christians have tended to shun the Old Testament. There are many theological considerations which require that attention be paid to the Old Testament. But, from the point of view of liberation preachers, there is also the question of the political setting of Scripture. The New Testament was written in a relatively brief time during which the church was a small minority with no access to political power. The Old Testament covers many more centuries, and in it we see the people of God enslaved, exiled, perplexed, and also relatively powerful. Therefore, questions of the proper ordering of society appear to be more clearly discussed in the Old Testament. Too often, however, under the guise of some such argument as that the New Testament is more "spiritual," such questions are shunned. And, even within the New Testament, some preachers have a tendency to preach on the Epistles of Paul, which they find easier to "spiritualize," than on the Gospels. The same is true of the general tendency to avoid narrative passages and choose those which seem to deal with "general" truths. In such a situation, the lectionary, with its assigned readings from the Old Testament as well as from the Gospels and the Epistles, should prevent the preacher from the pitfalls of a "spiritualistic" interpretation of the biblical message.

Avoidance, however, does not take place only in the selection of texts, but also in the way they are interpreted. There are three common ways in which this is done.

The first we have already discussed when dealing with the lectionary, and it has to do with the way texts are cut. Obviously, it is impossible to preach on the entire Bible, and therefore it is necessary to stop at some point. But what the preacher of liberation soon learns is that such cutting may in itself be a means of avoiding a portion of the text which traditional theology—both liberal and conservative —finds uncomfortable. Therefore, a good practice for a liberation preacher is always to ask, how would this text look if it were cut at another place? In some cases, this may simply mean refusing to leave out a few verses which the lectionary omits. But in other cases it may be to continue reading further in the text to keep its connection with verses that are usually read as entirely separate. We have already mentioned the fact that the parable of the Good Samaritan and the episode of Mary and Martha stand back to back in Luke 10. Another interesting exercise would be to preach on the parable of the Talents (Matt. 25:14-30), not by itself, but continuing the text to the end of the chapter. When thus read, the passage of the sheep and the goats does not appear as a separate one, but rather as the explanation of the parable. Then the parable takes a very different meaning than the one commonly ascribed to it, that the Lord wants us to use whatever talents we have.

A second means of avoidance consists in reading a text and dwelling on a part of it, while ignoring and perhaps even contradicting the rest. This takes place very often on Mothers' Day when preachers read Proverbs 31:10-31 and then wax eloquent on what a "good wife" is (by the way, the word "good" should actually be translated as "strong" or "courageous"), without paying any attention to what the rest of the text says. She is one who "considers a field and buys it; with the fruit of her hands she plants a vineyard. She girds her loins with strength and makes her arms strong" (vv. 16-17). This is not the meek, submissive, and supportive wife of many a sermon, who waits at home for her husband to take his shoes off when he comes in and makes him feel strong in contrast to her weakness.

To avoid this, the liberation preacher should always ask what is the part of the text that is usually ignored, and how the text actually looks when that part is restored to it. Take for instance the story of Peter's denial in Matthew 26:69-75. When we read this text asking what it is that usually goes unnoticed, what stands out is the reason why Peter was recognized as a follower of Jesus: "Certainly you are also one of them, for your accent betrays you" (Matt. 26:73). When we come across these words, we begin to suspect that part of what was involved in the trial and crucifixion of Jesus was the contempt of the people in Jerusalem for those of Galilee. And then we note that on the two previous occasions Peter has been questioned about his connection with "Jesus the Galilean" and with "Jesus of Nazareth." In the parallel texts in the other two synoptics (Mark 14:66-72 and Luke 22:54-62) the reference to Peter's accent does not appear; but, once we begin suspecting them, other regionalistic overtones are also present. Thus, what we have here is another indication of the socio-political factors which led to the crucifixion. Peter was being harassed and questioned, not because he acted like a follower of Jesus or because his face showed that he knew the Master, but because he was a foreigner, because he belonged to the same despised group as did Jesus.

A third means of avoidance is allegorical interpretation. This is more subtle when, rather than interpreting an entire passage allegorically, it simply does so with that part of the text which would be bothersome were it to be taken literally. We have already pointed out that those who argued for slavery on the basis of the Epistle to Philemon interpreted Paul's instruction to Philemon, that he was to receive Onesimus back "as a brother," in a "spiritual" sense, while they took literally the instruction to take him back. Another case in point has to do with the words of Jesus to the effect that it is easier for a camel to go through the eye of a needle than for a rich person to enter the kingdom (Matt. 19:24, Mark 10:25; Luke 18:25). The Armenian version, Cyril of Alexandria, and some rather late Greek manuscripts substituted the word "cable" *(kamilos)* for "camel" (*kamelos*), thus making it a little easier for the rich person to enter the kingdom. In the fifteenth century, an interpretation appeared according to which there was a gate called "the eye of the needle," and the only way a camel could go through it was by kneeling. The words of Jesus were then taken to mean that a rich person could enter the kingdom only by being humble. Biblical scholars have rejected both of these interpretations as being no more than attempts to get around what seem exceedingly hard words on Jesus' part. And yet, such interpretations continue to circulate among preachers, who find it convenient to avoid the harshness of what the Gospels tell us that Jesus said.

Another case in point is the interpretation of the psalms. We have already mentioned that in preaching on the 23rd Psalm the "enemies" are usually glossed over, or interpreted metaphorically as referring to our temptations. This is a symptom of the greatest difficulty many preachers have when dealing with the psalms. Many psalms sound rather vindictive and warlike. Therefore, preachers and liturgists choose those sections which are "nice" and leave out all that shows that many of these psalms express the hope of the oppressed and the despised that God will vindicate them. And yet, that hope is so central to the faith of Israel—and of the church—that to deny it or to set it aside is to miss a fundamental element in that faith.

In some cases such metaphorical interpretation seems to be warranted by the text. The best known example is Matthew 5:3, where Jesus says, "Blessed are the poor in spirit, for theirs is the kingdom of heaven." It has often been pointed out that the parallel text in Luke 6:20 does not speak of the "poor in spirit," but rather of "you poor." And then interpreters go on to say that Matthew has made it clear that Jesus was not referring to the materially poor, but rather to those who have the spirit of poverty and humility. To put it bluntly, it is claimed that Matthew means to say that Jesus was not really speaking of the poor, and that therefore it makes no matter how rich one is, as long as one is poor in spirit. It is a shame that the words "in spirit" have come to mean "untrue," and that when we say that something is "spiritually so," what we actually mean is that it really is not so. But it seems an unwarranted assumption to charge the Gospel of Matthew with such use of the phrase "in spirit"—or, in a more literal translation, "in the spirit" or "in the Spirit." There is no suggestion here that "in spirit" is intended to take away from the material reality of poverty. Actually, "at the time of Jesus, the term 'poor' is never used in a merely figurative sense, independent of social class."[5] When we look at the entire Bible, what we find is that material poverty is a very spiritual thing. This is not to say that poverty is good. It means rather that, since poverty is caused by oppression, God is on the side of the poor. For this reason the terms "poor" and "righteous" had come to have similar meaning. The poor within Israel, precisely because they are oppressed and God judges in their favor, are "in the Spirit." To claim, as is often done, that "the poor in spirit" means, not those who are materially poor, but those whose spirits act as if they were poor is to introduce a wedge between the material and the spiritual which is foreign to the Bible—a wedge which is very convenient for the rich and the powerful who gain their assurance by being told that all they have to do is to be poor and humble inside.

All of these pointers on biblical interpretation lead back to the "ideological suspicion" which is the hallmark of the liberation interpreter, and without which there is no liberation theology. They are not "principles of interpretation" which will guarantee a proper understanding of the text. There is no such principle in liberation theology, except the actual involvement in God's liberating actions—praxis—and the hermeneutical suspicion that comes out of it.

V. THE DYNAMICS OF LIBERATION PREACHING

Most of us assume that if we wish to know what a word means, a look in the dictionary will answer our question. Obviously, this is true as far as definitions are concerned. But as to what is communicated by that word, we need to look at more than the dictionary. Words do not stand alone. They are spoken by one person and addressed to another. The social relationship, the dynamic of power that exists between speaker and hearer in the wider society, makes an enormous difference as to exactly what is communicated. It is not enough to know the words. For instance, listen to these words: "Be satisfied with what you have. Do not be greedy." We can easily know what they mean in the abstract. Yet if we imagine them spoken in a middle-class white church by a guest preacher who is the pastor of a poor black church, there would be something different communicated than were exactly the same words spoken by the pastor of an affluent white church while preaching in a poor black congregation. In the one case there is a clear rebuke given to those who already have more than others. In the other, the one who has more is rebuking the aspirations for equality that those who have less might develop. The problem grows even greater when the powerful have many more opportunities to address the powerless, than the powerless to address the powerful. Yet this is clearly the case, for the powerful control more media, publish more books, give more lectures, chair more committees, and financially support more causes than do the powerless. And on the rare occasions when the powerless are invited to address the powerful, it is often treated by the powerful as a charitable or liberal action on their own part. Little of a significant nature can be communicated under those circumstances.

McLuhan was right. In some sense "the medium is the message."[1] In the case of preaching, the medium includes the social, political, and economic identity of the preacher. The message is also shaped in part by the social, political, and economic identity of the congregation. We must raise the political question, not only about the characters in the biblical text, but also about the characters in the event of preaching itself.

Those who are part of various liberation movements, those who are usually considered powerless by society, are well aware of such dynamics in communication. The woman who preaches does not have to be told that her identity as female is going to be perceived by the congregation and will be a factor in interpreting what she says. The minority person will be equally conscious of the effect of ethnic identity on the hearing of the words. For both the woman and the minority person this sense of the significance of identity will be present whether they are speaking to a group composed of those who are like themselves or to a group of the powerful. Always it matters and is a factor. Yet many white, male preachers remain oblivious to such considerations unless they are thrown into the situation of preaching in a minority church. The rest of the time, to be white and male seems to them to have no particular effect on the words spoken and heard. Yet that is not the case. In the act of preaching, the social and political situation of speaker and hearer are part of the context that gives meaning to the words that are spoken.

This is one of the reasons why both women and minority preachers are generally more biblical in their preaching than are many other people. They know quite well that when they preach, they have no status given them by society. In fact, the stereotypes are such that they realistically expect that they will be thought quite ignorant and incapable of conveying any significant message. Under such circumstances, aside from any theological opinion that would determine them to be biblical preachers, the explication and

application of a specific biblical text becomes their chief source of
authority in preaching, in a way and to a degree that is not necessary
for the white, male preacher. The white male preacher has general
credibility until he shows himself incompetent. Therefore, he may
be tempted to rely on public presence, jokes, irrelevant illustrations,
voice characteristics, and so forth, and not on the biblical text itself.
Those to whom society gives no such initial credibility find that they
cannot rely on such extraneous matters. Their only authority will be
in the biblical text, which must come through clearly and
unambiguously in their preaching. Only then can they expect a
hearing. White males who decide to preach on the radical demands
of Scripture as seen by liberation theology may soon find themselves
in a similar situation. This is one of the reasons why liberation
theology can lead to a biblical renewal in the task and art of
preaching.

THE POWERLESS WHO ARE PRESENT

Though our churches are frequently composed of only one race
and ethnic group, though they frequently reflect a limited spectrum
in terms of economic status, they are all composed of both men and
women, and the factor of power and powerlessness between the sexes
is present in all of them. Many of the women are currently struggling
with the issue of their own liberation, in a strong or hesitant fashion.
The fact that the preacher is male and much of the congregation is
female means that the words of the speaker will probably convey
something very different to many of the women than what they
convey to most of the men who hear the same sermon. A pastor who
is aware of such dynamics can make the communication far clearer
and avoid being misunderstood, by either the powerful or the
powerless in the congregation.

For instance, a male preacher may preach on Mark 8:34 and stress
the need to be selfless, to be constantly in the service of others rather
than concerned for ourselves. Of course there is truth to this
message. It is a necessary and central element of the gospel. These
words will probably be heard by many men as the pastor intends.
However, if a woman in the congregation is considering returning to

school and is struggling with the issue of how this will affect the family, she will probably hear these words as a rebuke to her new sense of possibility for herself. Her plans are selfish and therefore unchristian. She must continue to serve her family in the old way and not think about herself. At the same time, for that woman, the presence of a woman in the pulpit, no matter what she says, may in itself be a call and an inspiration to explore her own unknown capabilities.

Do we wish to equate Christian self-denial with the traditional role of the powerless? Are we really wishing to claim that subservience should continue and that any thought of self-determination is sinful? Surely that is not the case. Nor were the male pastor's words intended to reinforce the traditional roles and curb change. In fact, he may have thought his words would have the opposite effect and serve to rebuke the rest of the family for loading the work on the wife and mother. One of the most frequent breakdowns in communication comes when the powerful are rebuked from the pulpit by a pastor who is one of their number. Truly prophetic preaching needs to do this rebuking on occasion. But the same words, if there is no clear awareness of the political dimensions, can have the effect of saying to the powerless who hear the message that it is sinful to try to alter the status quo. What is implied is that as Christians they must stay in their place. A few direct comments could avoid such misunderstanding. The preacher can indicate for what human condition the message is appropriate. Possible mistaken understandings can be explicitly rejected. Only if the preacher is aware of these political dynamics within the congregation is the danger avoided. The use of clear contemporary examples that do not perpetuate stereotypes is another way of lessening such misunderstandings.

The matter is complicated by the fact that people cannot be simply identified as powerful or powerless. We have mentioned this before, and yet it must constantly be kept in mind by the liberation preacher. The white woman struggling for new possibilities still must remember that she is also an oppressor when it comes to the Third World or ethnic minorities within her own society. The same awareness of being cast in the role of oppressor by the Third World must be there for the minority person in our country. Even the white, male, middle-class American is in a way caught and oppressed. Liberation theology will function helpfully in a congregation only if the myriad of political dynamics present there is made clear and addressed by the gospel. A blanket pronouncement lacks the historical particularity that is one of the hallmarks of liberation theology itself. That specificity must be done by the preacher or the use of such theology is at best irrelevant and at worst oppressive.

Since women are the clearest example of the traditionally powerless who are present in most of our congregations, the issue of gender-specific language cannot be avoided. Obviously, language is more directly related to the women's movement than to any other liberation group. Gender problems arise in every language, but English has its own peculiarities. There are many books and articles that offer suggestions for correcting the constant use of "man," "mankind," etc., as though these words necessarily included women. There has also been significant work done on the alternatives to the constant use of masculine imagery and pronouns for God. These books and articles also give the rationale for such changes. It is not necessary here to dwell on the specifics of the language changes that are needed. Suffice it to say that the male pastor who does use inclusive language, who does acknowledge the validity of the issue, has taken a political stand that will be noticed and supported by those in the congregation who are struggling with the need for new roles for women. Conversely, any male pastor who does not make changes in his language is also communicating a political message of support for the traditional oppressive arrangement, whether he is conscious of this or not. The congregation will be quite aware of either message. It is out of this awareness that so much emotion is expended by those who do and do not want change. The preacher has no choice but to take a stand. The content of what is said will be interpreted partly by the context provided by the choice of language. That is to say, a male pastor who thinks he is quite liberating in his preaching and yet whose language remains unreconstructed will find that a certain skepticism greets his statements, whereas a pastor who does use altered language will be given the benefit of the doubt by those women who feel oppressed, even when some of his statements could otherwise be misinterpreted.

Changing language is not enough for liberation preaching, but exclusive language can blunt such preaching disastrously, at least as far as women are concerned, and they are the largest powerless group present in most congregations.

All that has been said refers to the male preacher. The female minister is not in quite the same situation. Obviously it is to be hoped and expected that she will use inclusive language. This will generally be the case. But if she does not, the fact of who she is, a woman in the pulpit, speaks so loudly against the traditional stereotypes of what women should be that her political stance in regard to women is still very different from that of a man who uses masculine language. She will still be viewed as supportive of their liberation, while the male minister would not be.

THE POWERLESS WHO ARE ABSENT

Many white, middle-class preachers have become interested in liberation theology, and yet some of the most significant powerless groups whose situation they hope to address are, almost by definition, not present in their congregations on Sunday morning. Their absence is explained by several obvious reasons. First of all, one group is probably Third World people who simply live on another part of the globe. Their absence is hardly surprising. A second group may well be those of ethnic minority or low socio-economic groups who live in the neighborhood but who do not attend the middle-class church. Obviously, some of these people may well be members of other congregations. Then the issue is how churches in a community can have positive relationships with one another across racial and economic lines, rather than how these people can change their local church membership. There may well be situations where a white congregation and pastor see the need for evangelism and mission in their own local area among unchurched people who would be classified by the society as marginal and powerless. With such a goal, a pastor may discover that preaching geared to the powerful, even the repentant powerful, may be alienating and oppressive to any member of the powerless group who happens to attend a service. Here again, as in the case of the women in the congregation, the preacher must be well aware of the political dynamics that affect how what the preacher says will actually be heard by the various members of the congregation, given their concrete situations, and given also the social status of the pastor who speaks the words. The powerless may be absent precisely because they know that they are not taken seriously when they are present. One goes to church to hear the gospel preached to one's own condition, not to overhear it preached to others.

The actual preaching heard by the rare member of a powerless group who attends the service is not the major way in which preaching relates to the absent powerless. The mission of the church in the world is not carried out primarily by the preacher from the pulpit. Yet the mission of the church is not totally divorced from that preaching either. From the standpoint of liberation theology, one of the major tasks that must be done in congregations composed of groups classified as powerful is to have such congregations develop an awareness of how they are viewed by the powerless. The mission of the church cannot be carried out authentically until there is such an understanding. This is most particularly true at present between the churches that have traditionally sent missionaries and the younger churches in the Third World. It is equally true in our own country between white churches and those of ethnic minorities. A sensitive preacher can help a congregation enormously in this respect.

This means that part of the task of preaching, as well as part of the preparation for it, is to ask the question, how would this biblical text be heard and applied authentically by someone in a radically different political and social setting? It is not only the preacher who needs to be aware of such interpretations in order to develop a more adequate theology; the congregation needs to develop the same skill in order to discover more adequately its mission in the world and how that mission can be carried out. The congregation is not helped unless the preacher uses some very clear examples. This is another way of reassigning the cast of characters in the text, as was discussed in the last chapter.

For instance, think about the parable of the workers in the vineyard, all of whom receive the same wage though they have labored very different amounts of time (Matt. 20:1-16). Most people in most congregations in the United States find this a text to avoid. It runs against our grain and seems quite unfair. We can probably understand that in regard to God all of us are those who were hired late, who have received from God far more than we deserve. But we prefer the way the parable of the Prodigal Son makes the same point. Yet when we imagine a group of Chicano migrant workers, waiting at the appointed place to be hired, perhaps, for the day, the parable begins to look quite different. For those who frequently find no work, for those who never know in the morning if there will be any wages at the end of the day, the parable would communicate the great justice, not the unfairness of God. The congregation needs to see this, and by so doing, the absent powerless will be brought into their midst.

Furthermore, once this aspect of the text is seen, then it becomes easier to see the relation of this particular parable to its setting in Matthew. Is it accidental that it follows immediately on a section (Matt. 19:16-30) that begins with the rich young ruler and ends with the disciples concerned about whether it was worthwhile to give up all they had in order to follow Jesus? Between these two stand the harsh words about how hard it is for the rich to enter the Kingdom. Both the section in Matthew 19 and the parable in 20 end with the cryptic words about the first being last, and the last first.

The presence in the sermon and therefore in the minds of the congregation of those migrant workers can begin to make clear where many of the rest of us fit into the text. The place of those whom the landlord rewards is taken by these others, and we are left in the more difficult situation of being the ones rebuked because we begrudge the generosity of the landlord. How do we respond to the rebuke? Do we feel that we deserve it? What does this say about how we ought to live out our faith in the world? Our dislike of the parable can then be understood and dealt with. It is a text that comes to life much more readily when the absent powerless are brought into the presence of the congregation.

It would be far easier for most of us if the church were limited to our own nation. Then we could avoid the situation of having the same Bible read and meditated upon by those who see us as their enemies or oppressors because of the economic and political relationships of our nation and its economy to those of the poorer countries of the world. It would be easier if those who are hungry did not include Christians who feel that we, their fellow Christians, are in some ways the cause of their hunger. But since these unpleasant facts are a reality, we are faced with the situation that many Christians in other parts of the world, as they read their Bibles and identify readily with the oppressed and the downtrodden, place us in the role of the enemies in the text. We cannot ignore their interpretation, but rather must seek to determine the justice of their reaction and ways to overcome both the reality and the hostility that ensues. We are indeed called to be part of the same Body of Christ, united by one faith, one baptism, and one Lord. The political situation in which we find ourselves destroys that unity much more than many of the differences in doctrine that have divided the church in the past. Our mission as the church is hindered in the world because of these political factors. Were we ever as the church able to reestablish our communication across these political lines, were we able to come to agreement as to what is actually the truth about our relationship to one another in the present world, the church could be a dynamic force for peace in the whole world and its message would be convincing. But in reality, we Christians are as much divided by the political dynamics of our time as are any other people. If in a local congregation our brothers and sisters in the faith who now stand in such a hostile relationship to us were actually made present, if we could begin to see the gospel from their point of view, then actually reestablishing links with them would be far more of a possibility. The preacher of liberation has more opportunity to make this a reality that does almost any one else within the church.

There seems to be a common model of preaching today that concerns itself only with the needs of those who are physically present in the congregation. This is seen as primarily pastoral. Obviously, the spiritual and material needs of the visible congregation need to be taken into consideration by the preacher. However, where the needs of those present are the main focus of preaching, the needs of those who are absent are missing, and the whole concept of the mission of the church is lost.

The relation of power and missions is complex. Yet it is true to say that in the past five or six hundred years, the branches of the Christian church that have developed missionary consciousness have been precisely in those countries that were beginning to make their power felt in the rest of the world: Spain and Portugal in the sixteenth century, England and the United States in the nineteenth and twentieth centuries. Part of the reason is that world-consciousness developed within the church in nations where the society was experiencing its own expansion into other parts of the globe. There also was money for such missionary ventures as the society expanded economically and politically.

This means, however, that as the issues of power and powerlessness become acute between First and Third World nations today, relationships are complicated between the churches that once sent missionaries and those that were founded by those missionaries in the past. In our own churches in the United States, the issue of what the overseas mission of the church ought to be and how it should be carried out has been both critical and divisive in the past few years. Very often there seems to be a breakdown in communication between boards of mission at the national level and local congregations. National boards are generally aware of the radically changed circumstances in a world where many of the traditionally powerless peoples are demanding drastic alterations in the balance between nations and between churches. Often such new understandings at the national level are not communicated or else are rejected by local congregations which still see the world in an earlier framework, where our country sent missionaries, determined what they would do, and had great success. They see no reason to change now. In fact, whatever are the conditions causing such change must be demonic! Now these younger churches demand much more autonomy, and even suggest that it would be helpful if our church received missionaries from the powerless churches who clearly have a word to speak as to the meaning of the gospel in our day. Such words are very difficult for many Christians in this country.

The pastor whose preaching begins to accustom a congregation to hearing such words has made great strides in enabling the mission of the church to go forward in the midst of a very new reality in the world. Such preaching could also begin to heal divisions within denominations caused by differing world-views and assumptions. To bring the absent powerless into the sermon wherever they belong in the biblical text can have these effects.

THE LITURGICAL CONTEXT

One of the most difficult problems in planning any worship service is to maintain some kind of coherence and logic among the various parts of the service. The process is further complicated when a new theological perspective is introduced into the preaching and the rest of the liturgy continues on a very different track. This is a problem many pastors are faced with when they begin to be affected by liberation theology and to use it in their own preaching. When one finishes the sermon, the congregation rises and sings a hymn that almost undoes the theological direction of the sermon. One speaks of the strength we have been given in Christ and the promise of victory, and the hymn tells only of our weakness. Or perhaps the worst combinations of hymn and sermon are avoided, and yet one can find nothing in the hymnbook that is really appropriate. The choice then is made of the hymn that does the least damage. This is an exaggeration, but points to a problem many pastors face. Liturgy is conservative and traditional, almost by its very nature. Congregations and pastors alike resist drastic and frequent changes in this area.

Yet the conservative character of liturgy can also be its greatest value, and it can lend unexpected and helpful support to the preaching that is oriented toward liberation. Recall the periods in the church's own history when there was serious persecution, when the church was not allied with the powerful structures of the society. The hymns that come from such a period will often be surprisingly relevant to our own age. Luther's hymn "A Mighty Fortress" takes on new and dramatic meaning when it follows a sermon that has clearly spelled out the demonic structures under which we live, and the assurance we have been given that God's just Word and Kingdom will prevail. "We Gather Together to Ask the Lord's Blessing" is a classic from a period of bitter persecution of many Christians in

Holland. The black spirituals come from another situation of oppression. A reference book that gives the historical context of hymns can help greatly in reviving neglected hymns or showing the full implications of familiar ones that have lost their original bite. Setting the stage for a hymn by giving the congregation a brief introduction to it can also help to make it supportive of liberation.

The prayers present a somewhat different problem. For some churches many of the prayers are traditional, and there may be some difficulty in altering them. What is needed, from the perspective of liberation theology, is not a complete deletion of what is generally used, but rather the inclusion of a balancing perspective. Official prayers, as well as theology, have generally been written from the point of view of the powerful. Most especially is this obvious in the prayers of confession. All the political factors that were mentioned earlier in this chapter, the different meanings the same words can have when heard by the powerless rather than by the powerful for whom they were intended, come into play in prayers as well. For instance, thinking more highly of ourselves than we ought to think is a more typical sin of the powerful than of the powerless, who usually have problems with a low self-image and a sense that they probably cannot succeed at much of significance. The same prayer of confession that can genuinely convict a powerful person can have the negative and theologically inaccurate result of increasing the low self-esteem of the powerless. It is not that pride should never be confessed. Rather it should be made clear what is not meant by the words. Paralyzing humility needs to be confessed, as does fearfulness of taking God-given responsibility. Yet rarely do these appear in prayers of confession written by the powerful, since these are not the sins which generally tempt them. Our simple thanksgiving that remembers gratefully "all that God has given us" may look different to the dispossessed who are not the least bit sure God did give it to us. Rather, to their eyes, we and our society as a whole have taken much of what God had actually given to others.

The same sort of mixed group that was suggested for Bible study, a group that cuts across age, sex, and racial lines, might also be the place where new and adequate prayers could be written. The same exercises in imaginative reflection on how various powerless groups would respond to a biblical text can be employed in the creating of prayers as well. The absent powerless—as well as the present powerless—need to be in the minds of those who create the rest of the liturgy if it is to be helpfully combined with a sermon that has a liberation flavor.

The preacher of liberation may be tempted to avoid as much of the traditional liturgy as possible and concentrate only on contemporary issues. Such an avoidance is neither necessary nor useful. In fact, the more it can be shown that what is being emphasized by liberation theology is at the heart of the gospel, especially as it was understood in the earliest time of the church's history and at critical points in its development thereafter, the more helpful it will be to a congregation. We often try to discard all tradition because we assume that all centuries were alike. A longer view is much more useful.

Nowhere is this seen more clearly than in dealing with the liturgical year. We do not have to choose between speaking on Advent and Christmas or on contemporary oppression. A true understanding of the significance of the Incarnation is necessary for a sense of possibility in the present. God is not prevented from bringing in the Kingdom simply because there is not room in our inns. We have already mentioned the magi, but Epiphany means more than even that story. To become experts at seeing God's manifestations, to be committed to God's authentic mission, these are also part of that celebration. Lent takes on new meaning with a rededication of ourselves to the hard way of the cross that it symbolizes. Even Ash Wednesday could become a new highpoint in a life of discipleship for any congregation. The whole Lenten season, with its joining of penitence and expected victory, has strong connections to the lives of oppressors who are themselves powerless, a group that constitutes the congregations of so many of our churches The culmination of Lent in Good Friday and Easter speaks of the cost of discipleship, the price of sin, and yet the overwhelming and joyful victory that has actually begun in Jesus' resurrection. The Ascension points to Jesus' power, that continues even now over all other earthly forces, and his continued intercession for us. Pentecost celebrates the gift of the Spirit that empowers us and unites us, even in the midst of the present struggle. To dig to the heart of the meanings of the church's great celebrations is to probe the heart of the gospel itself. In its earliest understandings, when the church needed to hear an authentic, liberating word for itself, it developed these celebrations to remind it of the fullness of the gospel. That word is still liberating for us when we approach it, haunted by the struggles of our own time. No superficial celebrations are possible for struggling, faithful Christians.

Nor must a preacher of liberation interrupt such preaching and return to a traditional stance when the sacraments are to be celebrated. Again, glances at early tradition can be helpful. Baptism can be central, a time to remind all of us who we are, to whom we belong, and the significance that flows from such a life-long awareness. The Lord's Supper can become once again what it originally was, the great Thanksgiving for the victory won for us in the Cross and the Resurrection. Let it be the celebration of the presence of the Crucified and Risen Lord in the midst of his people, giving them forgiveness, new strength, new possibilities, and new life. Let it be the foretaste of the coming Kingdom.

To be a preacher of liberation can make one also the rediscoverer of some of the greatness of the liturgical tradition. Much of present worship does need to be altered. But this can often best be done by a renewal of some of the authentic tradition that has been neglected, and not by abandoning all that has gone before. The liturgical context must be taken into account by the preacher of liberation, as well as by any other preacher. The same viewpoint needs to be taken regarding it as has been taken regarding the exposition of the biblical text itself.

VI. THE LIBERATING PROCESS

Throughout this book we have centered our attention on preaching and on the biblical interpretation which stands at its base. This, however, should not obscure the fact that there can be no liberation preaching without actual involvement in the process of liberation. This is why we have repeatedly dealt with the "ideological suspicion" which lies at the base of all liberation exegesis. That suspicion is not a methodology which one learns in the classroom—although many women and ethnic minorities can point to classroom experiences which helped awaken that suspicion. It is rather the result of involvement in a liberation movement with the consequent discovery that the ideological dice are loaded, such that many of those things which appear to be neutral are in fact hidden supports for an oppressive system. And this goes for theology and preaching at least as much as it goes for anything else. It is that ideological suspicion that provokes the creativity of liberation theologians and preachers, as well as of liberation historians, educators, and others. Without it, all one can do is mouth what others have said.

The liberation theologians whom we have quoted in this book have all gone through that process. Some are Roman Catholic priests whose work in the slums of Latin America convinced them that the problems were much deeper than they had been told, and that a systemic change was required, not only in politics and economics, but also in theology and in the life of the church. Others are North American blacks and women who have known the pain of the limitations set on them by the surrounding culture and out of that pain have developed their own ideological suspicion. All of them are highly trained theologians and scholars, who were able therefore to turn the tools that they had, not only against oppression in general, but also against oppression in academic theology. This is the path that anyone who hopes to be a liberation preacher must tread.

This does not mean that one must necessarily be an activist. In fact, it may be that a great deal of activism of the clergy in decades past was in part a means whereby the laity evaded facing up to the full implications of the gospel. During the height of the Viet Nam war, there were many preachers involved in the protests. Their courage should not be denied, especially at the time when the war was still relatively popular. But what should also be remembered is that behind each of those preachers there were hundreds of parishioners who supported them financially, who thought that what they were doing was a genuine concern of the Christian conscience, but who were never seen in the protests, never risked the goodwill of their neighbors, and never scandalized their business acquaintances. The same may be said of the participation of many white preachers in the civil rights movement.

In short, ideological suspicion must also be applied to political activism on the part of preachers, lest the preacher who is at the picket line take the place of a hundred parishioners who ought to be there. The preacher must be an active participant in the movement of liberation; but when this becomes the sort of activism which takes responsibility off other people's shoulders, it must be redirected. Or one could say that the reason for a preacher's activity in favor of liberation is not ordination, but baptism—a baptism which commits us, and all Christians, to seek that which is most truly human, not only for and with other believers, but also for and with the entire human race.

Another point to keep in mind is that there is only one liberation, and that therefore there is only one oppression. In a sense, this is a theological statement, made on the basis of faith. The basic tenet of the Christian faith is that the victory is the Lord's, and that through that victory he is our redeemer. "For there is no other name given to humans under heaven by which we may be saved" (Acts 4:12). But this also implies that the powers of oppression which he has defeated and is defeating are in the final analysis only one. There is only one Victor, and there is only one Enemy.

Although this statement is based on faith, observation of the present world order seems to confirm it. Racism in the United States is not unrelated to apartheid in South Africa, and the two are supported by the same economic structures which lead to the dispossession of peasants in Brazil and the Philippines. The exploitation of women, their stereotyping into sex roles or into Christmas trees on which successful males display the signs of their success, is also part of the same picture. The fear which white males in the United States manifest toward their black and Hispanic counterparts is the other side of the coin of the way in which women are stereotyped in their own society. And minority men are often led by their own oppression to oppress minority women. All of this is closely related to our present consumer society, where human beings are seen as either means of production or agents of consumption, and where the poor are valued according to how much they produce, and the rich according to how much they consume.

The consequence of this unity of the oppressive system is that to strike a blow for any particular kind of liberation is to strike a blow against the system itself. And this is the reason why it is possible to preach and practice liberation even though one is a white middle-class male preacher in the United States. It is possible, because the liberation of the middle-class will eventually be part of the entire process of liberation of the human race. But it is also difficult, because the middle-class lives precisely by the myth that it is not oppressed. It is easier to convince a successful businessman that he is an oppressor, than to convince him that he is oppressed. The reason for that should be quite obvious. If that businessman becomes convinced that he is an oppressor he still has that sense of power which is so important for his own image of himself. But if he is told that he is oppressed this means that all the tokens of his success, with which the system rewards him, are little more than the price paid for his enslavement. He is little more than more meat for the grinder of production. And it is difficult for a middle-class, white male to admit this.

Furthermore, it is difficult, because the price to be paid for such admission could be exceedingly high. That businessman may admit that he is psychologically oppressed and go to a psychiatrist seeking a solution, but to admit the kind of oppression of which we are talking here may lead to radical changes in life-style and to eventual expulsion from the middle class.

The same point could be made by means of a comparison that may at first seem shocking. The middle class is to the present order in the United States what the army is to dictatorships in Latin America. The soldiers in such a dictatorship lord it over the people, and from the point of view of the people they are the oppressors. But these soldiers know quite well that they cannot do as they please, that no matter how guilty they feel about it they have to apply the repressive orders of the regime. They have to do this, first of all, because were the regime to topple most of those who are really close to the dictator will simply leave the country, but the soldiers will have to stay, and therefore they will be the hardest hit. They also have to do it because they know that were they simply to resign from the army someone else would come to take their place, and they would be left in the unenviable position of being neither in the army nor with the people who suffer under it. Furthermore, the dictatorship would act more severely against them than against the common people, for fear that their attitude would spread, and the army would melt away. Thus, soldiers in such a situation are placed in the difficult position of being powerless oppressors. To realize that they are oppressors may give them an uneasy conscience, but to admit that they are powerless and oppressed would cost them their livelihoods, and probably their lives.

Most of the "successful" men in our congregations are in the same situation. Without them as a group the system cannot survive. And precisely for that reason the system rewards them and seeks to hide their oppression. But were they to come to consciousness, the price for their rebellion would be very high. This is why a white male liberation movement has scarcely developed, and in those places where it has appeared it has tended to limit itself to issues of relations with females and their liberation, but has refused to pose the larger questions of the economic order of which such males are a part.

This is also the reason why it is so difficult to be a liberation preacher in a middle-class congregation. It may be possible to speak of the liberation of others; but that is not what liberation preaching requires. It may be possible to speak of inner oppression, and liberation from it; but that is not all that liberation preaching must address. To be a liberation preacher in such a setting is to embark on a long and costly journey, with no guarantee that those who are traveling with you really wish to travel that road—and perhaps not even that you yourself wish to travel it.

Finally, the unity of oppression and of liberation means that liberation is a process rather than a state, at least till the Kingdom comes. There is a great deal of talk about "liberated" men and women. Such language is not very helpful, since it would seem to imply that liberation is only an inner attitude or one that is limited to one's direct relations with those with whom one interacts most often. And it is true that liberation has a great deal to do with all this, but liberation is not something which I can have by myself. It is not an inner state of mind. It is not having the consciousness that there is a great deal in our society which has to be changed. The consciousness is necessary, for this is the basis of the ideological suspicion of which we have spoken so often. But that is only the starting point, and to turn it into the goal of liberation is to be guilty of the same tendency to internalize and individualize everything which has made so much of traditional theology so oppressive.

In theological terms, what this means is that we are speaking of the Kingdom. A theology of liberation is a theology of the Kingdom. The goal toward which we move is the fulfilment of the promises of the Kingdom. As citizens of that Kingdom, we must renounce service to the present order. We are Christ's, not Caesar's, and for that reason we refuse to give ourselves to Caesar. Since in Christ the Kingdom has come, we can now live out of that new order. But since he is also still to come, we are not yet liberated, but in the process of being liberated—or, in more familiar terms, of working out our own salvation with fear and trembling, for God is at work in us (Phil. 2:12).

To attempt to preach this liberation in our churches may be a very costly thing. But then, the gate is narrow, and the way is hard that leads to life.

NOTES

CHAPTER I: What is Liberation Theology?

1. See, for instance, Alfonso López Trujillo, *La liberación y el compromiso del cristiano ante la política* (Bilbao: Mensajero, 1973).

2. Albert Memmi, *The Colonizer and the Colonized* (Boston: Beacon Press, 1965).

3. Eusebius of Caesarea, *Church History*, 3.25.

4. Raúl Vidales, "El sujeto histórico de la teología de la liberación, "*Taller de teología, II: Praxis cristiana y producción teológica en América Latina* (México: Comunidad Teólogica de México, 1972), p. 9.

5. James H. Cone, *A Black Theology of Liberation* (Philadelphia: J. B. Lippincott, 1970), p. 53.

6. *Ibid.*, p. 93.

7. Letty M. Russell, *Human Liberation in a Feminist Perspective: A Theology* (Philadelphia: Westminster, 1974), p. 58.

8. Rosemary Reuther, *Liberation Theology: Human Hope Confronts Christian History and American Power* (New York: Paulist Press, 1972), p. 3.

9. Gustavo Gutiérrez, *A Theology of Liberation: History, Politics, and Salvation* (Maryknoll, N.Y.: Orbis Books, 1973), p. 10.

10. Cone, *Black Theology*, p. 95.

11. Russell, *Human Liberation*, p. 53.

12. James H. Cone, *God of the Oppressed* (New York: Seabury, 1975), pp. 30-31.

13. This may be seen, for instance, in the wide range of subjects discussed by Juan Luis Segundo in *A Theology for Artisans of a New Humanity* (Maryknoll, N.Y.: Orbis Books, 1973). The titles of the five volumes are: *The Community Called Church, Grace and the Human Condition, Our Idea of God, The Sacraments Today,* and *Evolution and Guilt.*

14. Cone, *Black Theology*, pp. 131-32.

15. "Most Christians would also find it surprising that more space in the Bible is devoted to regulating and limiting the rights of property than to regulating sexual

behavior. Most Christians would object much more strongly to the ordination of a homosexual than they would to that of a wheeler-dealer. And yet, Scripture has harsher words to say about the latter than it has to say about the former." J. L. González, "Searching for a Liberating Anthropology," *Theology Today*, 34:393.

16. One of the most interesting books written from the perspective of a white, middle-class, male American minister, who has discovered the bondage under which he has lived, is Richard Shaull's section of the work *Liberation and Change*, which also includes writings of Gustavo Gutiérrez (Atlanta: John Knox Press, 1977). Shaull writes: "In the midst of the turmoil of the Sixties, I was forced to face the fact that, for many of the most sensitive of a younger generation, *the American dream had become a nightmare*. Institutions which had offered me and my generation the hope of a better future, were now experienced as structures of death. . . . The American dream had died, not only for many others *but for myself as well*. . . . In the midst of the collapse of the old order, I see signs of a new world taking shape; I begin to perceive and to work for a *new* future." pp. 100-101.

CHAPTER II: Difficulties in Hearing the Text

1. Catherine G. González and Justo L. González, *Their Souls Did Magnify the Lord* (Atlanta: General Assembly Mission Board, Presbyterian Church in the U.S., 1977).

2. Juan Luis Segundo, *The Liberation of Theology* (Maryknoll, N.Y.: Orbis Books, 1976), p. 9.

3. William L. Wonderly, *Bible Translations for Popular Use* (New York: United Bible Societies, 1968), p. 51.

4. See, for instance, the articles *adelphos* and *pater* in William F. Arndt and F. Wilbur Gingrich, *A Greek–English Lexicon of the New Testament* . . . (University of Chicago Press, 1957).

5. James W. Cox, ed., *The Twentieth Century Pulpit* (Nashville: Abingdon, 1978).

CHAPTER III: The Forgotten Interpreters

1. *Ep. ad Smyrnaeos*, 6.2 (BAC 65:492). This quotation as well as most of those that follow, and hundreds of others, may be found in: Juan Leuridán, ed., *Justicia y explotación en la tradición cristiana antigua* (Lima: Centro de Estudios y Publicaciones, 1973) and in the more extensive collection by R. Sierra Bravo, *Doctrina social y económica de los padres de la iglesia* (Madrid: Compañía Bibliográfica Española, 1967).

2. *Simil.*, 10.4.2-3 (BAC 65:1091).

3. *De Nabuthe Jezraelita*, 1.1 (PL 14:767).

4. *De officiis ministrorum*, 1.28.132 (PL 16:62).

5. *De Nab. Jez.*, 1.11 (PL 14:783).

6. *Expositio Evangelii secundum Lucam*, 7.124 (PL 15:1731).

7. *De Nab. Jez.*, 1.3 (PL 14:769).

8. *Ibid.*, 1.1 (PL 14:767).

9. *Homilia in illud Lucam, Destruam* . . . , 7 (PG 31:277).

10. *Homilia de Lazaro*, 2.6 (PG 48:992).

11. *Homilia in Psalmum xiv* (PG 29:273).
12. *Homilia in divites*, 5 (PG 31:293).
13. *Epistola cxx* (PL 22:984).
14. *De justitia*, 5 (PL 11:286).
15. *Enarratio in Psalmum cxxxi* (PL 37:1718).
16. *Divinarum Institutionum libri septem*, 5.5 (PL 6:565).
17. *Comment. in Lucam v.x* (PG 72:816).
18. *Regulae Pastoralis liber*, 3.21 (PL 77:87).
19. *In Ep. I ad Thimoteum*, 4.12.3 (PG 62:562).
20. *Ibid.*, 4.12.4 (PG 62:563).
21. *Homilia de Lazaro*, 6.8 (PG 48:1039).
22. *In Mattaeum homilia lxxvii* (PG 58:708).
23. *In Joannem homilia lxv* 3 (PG 59.364).
24. *In Psalmum xlviii*, 3 (PG 55:517).
25. *De Poenitentia*, 7.7 (PG 49:335).
26. See, for instance, the startling words of John Wesley quoted by Ronald J. Sider, *Rich Christians in an Age of Hunger* (Downers Grove, Ill.: Intervarsity Press, 1977), pp. 172-73.
27. *In Ecclesiasten Salomonis homilia iv* (PG 44:665).
28. *On the Dress of Virgins*, 22 (ANF 5:436).
29. Ernesto Cardenal, *The Gospel in Solentiname* (Maryknoll, N.Y.: Orbis Books, 1976).
30. *Ibid.*, pp.15-16.
31. *Ibid.*, p. 18.
32. *Ibid.*, p. 62.
33. *Ibid.*, pp. 154, 152.
34. Letty M. Russell, ed., *The Liberating Word: A Guide to Nonsexist Interpretation of the Bible* (Philadelphia: Westminster Press, 1976), p. 62.
35. *Ibid.*, p. 65.
36. Rachel Conrad Wahlberg, *Jesus According to a Woman* (New York: Paulist Press, 1975), p. 44.
37. *Ibid.*, p. 65.
38. General H. Anderson and Thomas F. Stransky, eds., *Mission Trends No. 3: Third World Theologies* (New York: Paulist Press, 1976), pp. 152-54.

CHAPTER IV: Some Pointers on Biblical Interpretation

1. John Calvin, *Commentary on Joshua* (Grand Rapids: Eerdmans, 1949), p. 46.
2. Here is another instance in which the study of early Christian literature may be useful. There is a tradition of interpretation, which appears as early as Tertullian (*De idol.*, 15), that in this dialogue Jesus was contrasting the image of Caesar in the coin with that of God in humans. There is ample material for reflection along such lines, which would seem to imply that there is a tension between bearing the image of God and paying undue honor to that which bears the image of Caesar.
3. *Freedom Made Flesh: The Mission of Christ and His Church* (Maryknoll, N.Y.: Orbis Books, 1976), p. 80.
4. On the customs and laws regarding marriage, the authority of the *pater familias*, and slavery, see the articles "Marriage," "Manus," "Familia," "Emancipatio,"

"Freedmen," "Mancipium," "Coemptio," and "Slaves" in Oskar Seyffert, *Dictionary of Classical Antiquities*, edition revised by H. Nettleship and J. E. Sandys (New York: Meridian Library, 1956). For less detail, see Lionel Casson, *Daily Life in Ancient Rome* (New York: McGraw-Hill, 1975).

5. Eduard Schweizer, *The Good News according to Matthew* (Atlanta: John Knox Press, 1975), p. 86.

CHAPTER V: The Dynamics of Liberation Preaching

1. Herbert Marshall McLuhan, *Understanding Media: The Extensions of Man* (New York: McGraw-Hill, 1964).

FOR FURTHER READING

CHAPTER I: What is Liberation Theology?

Cone, James H. A Black Theology of Liberation. Philadelphia: J. B. Lippincott, 1970.
———. God of the Oppressed. New York: Seabury Press, 1975.
Gutiérrez, Gustavo, and Schaull, Richard. Liberation and Change. Atlanta: John Knox Press, 1977.
Gutiérrez, Gustavo. A Theology of Liberation: History, Politics and Salvation. Maryknoll, N.Y.: Orbis Books, 1973.
Miguez Bonino, José. Doing Theology in a Revolutionary Situation. Philadelphia: Fortress Press, 1975.
Reuther, Rosemary. Liberation Theology: Human Hope Confronts Christian History and American Power. New York: Paulist Press, 1972.
Russell, Letty M. Human Liberation in a Feminist Perspective; A Theology. Philadelphia: Westminster Press, 1974
Segundo, Juan Luis. A Theology for Artisans of a New Humanity. 5 vols. Maryknoll: Orbis Books, 1973.

CHAPTER II: Difficulties in Hearing the Text

Russell, Rosemary R., ed. Religion and Sexism: Images of Woman in the Jewish and Christian Traditions. New York: Simon and Schuster, 1974.
Segundo, Juan Luis. The Liberation of Theology. Maryknoll, N.Y.: Orbis Books, 1976.

CHAPTER III: The Forgotten Interpreters

Cardenal, Ernesto. The Gospel in Solentiname. 3 vols. Maryknoll, N.Y.: Orbis Books, 1976–79.

Leuridán, Juan. *Justicia y explotación en la tradición cristiana antiqua*. Lima: Centro de Estudios y Publicaciones, 1973.

Russell, Letty M., ed. *The Liberating Word: A Guide to Nonsexist Interpretation of the Bible*. Philadelphia: Westminster Press, 1976.

Santa Ana, Julio de. *Good News to the Poor: The Challenge of the Poor in the History of the Church*. Geneva: World Council of Churches, 1977.

Sierra Bravo, Restituto. *Doctrina social y económica de los padres de la iglesia*. Madrid: Compañía Bibliográfica Española, S.A. 1976.

Wahlberg, Rachel Conrad. *Jesus According to a Woman*. New York: Paulist Press, 1975.

CHAPTER IV: Some Pointers on Biblical Interpretation

Comblín, José. *Sent from the Father: Meditations on the Fourth Gospel*. Maryknoll, N.Y.: Orbis Books, 1979.

González, Catherine G., and González, Justo L. *Their Souls Did Magnify the Lord: Studies on Biblical Women*. Atlanta: General Assembly Mission Board of the Presbyterian Church, U.S., 1977.

CHAPTER V: The Dynamics of Liberation Preaching

Balasuriya, Tissa. *The Eucharist and Human Liberation*. Maryknoll, N.Y.: Orbis Books, 1979.

Emsweiler, Sharon Neufer, and Thomas Neufer. *Women and Worship: A Guide to Non-sexist Hymns, Prayers, and Liturgies*. New York: Harper & Row, 1974.

Reformed Liturgy and Music (Fall, 1974).

INDEX OF SUBJECTS AND AUTHORS

INDEX OF BIBLICAL REFERENCES